HOW TO KNOW
GOD'S WILL

HOW TO KNOW GOD'S WILL

By

MARION H. NELSON, M.D.

MOODY PRESS

CHICAGO

Printed in the United States of America

CONTENTS

PREFACE

THERE ARE A NUMBER OF MATTERS within Christianity that seem confusing and controversial. One is this matter commonly called "the Lord's will."

This area of Christianity is confusing in several ways. First, the term itself is sometimes not defined clearly or consistently.

Second, how one goes about determining the Lord's will for his life is frequently not known. Many are ignorant as to the correct procedure to be followed. Thus the methods used in determining God's will are often incomplete and haphazard, with inevitable incorrect results.

Third, the term is frequently used by some people to try to justify their own decisions and actions. To defend something they do, they simply label it "the Lord's will for me." They expect this to open up the way for them to have their own way, regardless, and thus avoid any criticism from the Lord or others. In other words, they try to use the term almost as a magical formula, which sanctifies anything they want. It is easy to say, "This is the Lord's will for me," but this doesn't make it true.

Fourth, there are many perplexing problems in applying general Biblical principles to specific life situations. It is sometimes difficult to be sure about the right decision from the Christian viewpoint. Here it is especially important to approach it objectively and use a thorough procedure.

In this book I have tried to concentrate upon the correct procedure the Christian should follow in determining the Lord's will for his life. This book can be used somewhat like the checklist a pilot uses before he takes off in his airplane. If his procedure has been careful, his flight is likely to be successful.

The Christian's motivation for wanting to do the Lord's will is not exactly my subject, but I feel it warrants some mention. There are several legitimate reasons. First, because we love Him (John 14:15, 21, 23-24) and want to please Him (I John 3:22). The desire to please someone you love is the most compelling of all. Second, because in return for our obedience we will receive blessing in this life (I Peter 3: 10-12) and rewards in the future life (I Corinthians 3:10-15; II Timothy 4:8; Heb. 10:35). To desire and expect rewards in Heaven is in no way inconsistent with one's wish to please God. The hope of future rewards held out by God to Christians who try to please Him is a legitimate and strong force. Third, to avoid chastening by the Lord in this life (I Cor. 3: 16-17; 11:31-32; I Peter 4:17). No one enjoys being chastened, yet we all need it because of our tendency to wander into that which is contrary to God's will. Fourth, to be a good example to other Christians (I Cor. 4:16; I Thess. 1:7; II Thess. 3:9; Heb. 13:7). Fifth, because in this way we will avoid being ashamed at Christ's second coming (I John 2: 28).

Such reasons ought to be sufficient to leave the Christian well motivated to know and to do the Lord's will. My prayer is that those who are well motivated will find this book helpful in discerning what is the will of the Lord.

Chapter 1

WHAT IS GOD'S WILL?

A. THE CHRISTIAN'S OBLIGATION TO KNOW GOD'S WILL

IN EPHESIANS 5:15 the Christian is commanded by Paul to conduct himself carefully (*akribōs,* accurately; see Matt. 2:8; Luke 1:3; Acts 18:25), not as unwise ones but as wise ones. The idea of the word "wise" (*sophos*) in this verse is "having the facts." Then in verse 16 the Christian is told to take advantage of every opportune time that comes along: that is, use every opportunity to do that which is good, considering how much evil there is. Then in verse 17 he is further instructed to stop being foolish, and this word for "foolish" (*aphrōn,* senseless, without reason) has the idea of one who "doesn't use the facts" and thus acts in a rash, foolish, or unintelligent manner.

The Christian is supposed to have the facts and to be careful in his behavior. He should use facts intelligently. Moreover, in verse 17 he is instructed to be understanding what the will (*thelēma,* a desire from the heart) of the Lord is. The word here for understand (*suniēmi*) has the idea of "bringing together," meaning, putting all the facts together and arriving at a sound, logical conclusion. We are to do this in regard to the will of the Lord. We are to collect all

9

the information available regarding the will of the Lord, put it together, and come to a sound conclusion as to what His will is.

One must first accurately determine what His will is if he is to correctly carry out His will. I believe that today all sorts of ridiculous and unintelligent things are being done, being labeled incorrectly as the Lord's will. The correct procedure for discerning His will has been neglected. To proceed in a haphazard way in determining something as important as this is inexcusable.

The main purpose of the book is to set forth the correct procedure for determining the Lord's will. But first I must define the term "Lord's will," so I can be sure the reader is thinking about the same concept I'm thinking of.

B. DEFINITION OF THE WORD "WILL"

There are several different words used in the New Testament translated as "will" and used to indicate the will of God. All have different meanings. It is important at this point for the reader to put aside his preconceived idea of what he thought the will of God meant. Instead he should try to understand the different concepts presented in the Bible through these words that are explained below.

First, we have words denoting God's purpose. God has an over-all plan or purpose which He is carrying out today in the world. In II Timothy 1:9 Paul says that God saved us (Christians) according to (that is, on the basis of) His own purpose and grace. The word for "purpose" here is *prothesis*. It is related to the verb *protithēmi*, which means to "set before oneself, to purpose." God "set before Himself" a goal or purpose to accomplish, and He is now bringing it to pass.

In Ephesians 1:9 Paul says that this purpose stemmed from God's "will" which was "according to His good pleasure." The word here translated as "good pleasure" (*eudokia*) has the idea of that which seems good or pleasing to God. It is related to the verb *eudokeō*, which means to "be pleased with something, to think something good."

God thought matters over and was pleased to accomplish certain things. Thus, He put these things before Himself to carry out. These things became part of His plan or purpose.

These things that seemed good to God were in turn related to God's "will" (Eph. 1:9). Here the word for "will" is *thelēma*, which refers to a "desire which stems from the heart." It is related to the verb *thelō*, which means "to desire something from the heart, to want."

To summarize, God has certain desires in His heart, certain things He wants to accomplish. He decided that it would be good if these things were accomplished in a certain way. Thus, He has purposed within Himself to bring these things to pass in that particular way. This purpose and the way in which it is to be accomplished is God's will in the sense of His "plan" or "purpose."

Now, in the previous paragraph I used the word "decide" in regard to God's pondering over His plan. While considering the wishes of His heart God did think things over in His mind and reach a decision about them. To perform this action of thinking things over and deciding and thus having a definite wish, stemming from the mind, is the idea of the verb *boulomai*, which means "to desire something from the mind, to decide." It is a stronger word than *thelō*. It includes the idea of determination and frequently should be translated as "plan" (see I Cor. 12:11; II Cor. 1:15; James 3:4). To contrast this word with *thelō*, one could say that *thelō* means "I want," while *boulomai* means "I decide or I plan." It is not wrong to translate it as "I will," but this does not demonstrate in English the idea of "deciding after pondering in the mind," which idea is inherent in the word.

Related to the verb *boulomai* is the noun *boulē*, which means "plan" or "decision" (see Acts 27:12). It is sometimes translated as "will." In Ephesians 1:11 Paul says that God is constantly working (that is, bringing to pass; literally, energizing) all things after (that is, on the basis of) the counsel (*boulē*, plan) of (that is, stemming from) His own will (*thelēma*, heart's desire).

To summarize, one can say that in order to fulfill the wishes (*thelēma*) of His heart God formulates a plan (*boulē*) which He is now carrying out. In Acts 2:23 and 4:28 Luke says that the crucifixion of Christ, as displeasing as it must have been to God the Father, nevertheless was according to the counsel (*boulē*, plan) of God.

In Hebrews 6:17 it is stated that God's counsel (*boulē*, plan) is unchangeable. Also, in Romans 9:19 it is stated that His will (*boulēma*, plan, intention, deliberate purpose; a word closely related to *boulē*) is irresistible. So then, that which is the Lord's will in the sense of *boulē* (plan) is inevitably accomplished. From Ephesians 1:11 we see that God is bringing to pass all things on the basis of His will (*boulē*, plan). Now, this plan includes many, but not all, of God's heart's desires (*thelēma*). That this is true is seen from I Timothy 2:4, where Paul says that God will have (*thelō*: literally, has a desire in His heart for) all men to be saved. God would like all men to accept Christ as their Saviour and be saved, but it is obvious that not all men do this. On the contrary, many men reject Christ and remain lost . Why God did not decide to make this particular wish (*thelēma*) part of His irresistible plan (*boulē*) is not revealed in the Bible. It is definitely related to the issue of permitting men to exercise what is popularly called "free will," which I think could more accurately be called "a conscious, deliberate choice for which a man is held responsible." In Romans 9:22 Paul says that God, although wanting (*thelō*) to manifest His anger and to make known His power, yet endured vessels of wrath. He permitted vessels of wrath in His plan (*boulē*), things that were displeasing to Him, in order to carry out His purpose mentioned in Romans 9:23.

On the basis of the above Biblical passages we, as Christians, must assume that God's plan (*boulē*) for our lives is fixed and unchangeable and will inevitably be done. To try to determine what this plan is for the future would be like trying to look into a crystal ball and be a miraculous prophet. We can't do it.

We need to remember that this plan for our lives includes the human processes of our being educated about God and our learning to use this knowledge in everyday living. Part of God's plan has to do with our efforts to find out what God wants (*thelō*) us to do, what city He wants us to live in, what work He wants us to do, what house He wants us to live in, and similar things. His plan includes both our successes and failures. Why would God include a failure in His plan for our lives? Because we can learn from our mistakes.

So then, for the purpose of this book, we may define our use of the term, God's will, as God's *thelēma* (His wish). We are not talking about what we are destined to do within God's sovereign plan, but rather what God wants us to do.

Sometimes we will be successful and sometimes we will fail in doing what He wants us to do. This use of *thelēma* for God's will is well illustrated in the following verses: Matthew 21:31, where only one of the two sons did what his father wanted him to do; I Corinthians 16:12, where Apollos did not want to go to Corinth at that time; I Thessalonians 4:3-6, where God indicates that He wants our sex life to be sanctified in the sense of its being limited to the marital partner and not being defiled by fornication or adultery. Within the limits of marriage God says that there is no defilement in sex (see Heb. 13:4). In Acts 16:7 Paul wanted to go to Bithynia, but the Holy Spirit did not allow him to, indicating that God did not want Paul to go there at that time. So, in this book, the will of God refers to what God wants us to do.

Chapter 2

HOW DOES GOD MAKE KNOWN HIS WILL?

A. THROUGH THE WORD OF GOD

A LARGE PORTION of what God wants from us is revealed in the Bible. For instance, regarding such things as murder, adultery, and robbery there is clear instruction that God does not want us to do these things.

There are some other issues about which the Bible gives only principles, which must be understood and properly applied in order to reach a decision consistent with what God wants. An example is the need for separation and the principle of not being unequally yoked with unbelievers (see II Cor. 6:14). Another example is the general principle that every man, if physically and emotionally able, is to labor at some occupation (I Thess. 4:11-12; II Thess. 3:10-12). The Bible does not reveal what kind of work each man is to do, such as farming or banking. This we have to determine as the Spirit of God leads us. Such things as what kind of work we are to do, what city we are to live in, what kind of car we are to drive, and what house we are to buy, are not revealed in the Bible. Yet Biblical principles should help us in determining what God wants us to do about such matters. How does God communicate this part of His will to us?

B. THROUGH CONTROL OF ONE'S THOUGHT LIFE

Romans 8:7 tells us that the mind does not naturally place itself in subjection to the law of God. It is thus necessary for God to do something toward influencing our minds in the direction He wants. In what ways can He exert such control?

1. By Indirect Control of One's Thought Life

God can exercise an indirect control over our minds by maintaining principles, psychological in nature, which regulate the functioning of the mind. Since He controls circumstances which produce psychological effects upon us, and since He controls the principles governing the mind's functioning, He can thus control the mind.

The existence of these psychological principles and related physiological laws governing brain function make possible the science of psychiatry. A given conscious thought can frequently be traced back and found to be the end result of a series of other thoughts, both conscious and subconscious, all operating according to definite patterns. By knowing all of our conscious and subconscious thoughts, God would be able to know how we would respond to a given situation. He could anticipate what thoughts and feelings we would have.

Trials or testings are an example of this type of control. In a test or trial a Christian is put under stress and perhaps will experience emotions such as frustration or sorrow. Therefore, as a result of the trial, he will have certain thoughts and feelings. Of course, God has a good reason for sending a test. He has in mind the further maturation of the person (see II Cor. 7:8-11; 12:7; I Peter 1:6-7; 4:12-13; James 1:2-4).

God may lead us about geographically by utilization of our human thought tendencies and behavior patterns. For instance, He may so order circumstances in the city where we are living that we become so unhappy that we begin thinking of moving to a different city. It was through the suffering accompanying the persecution of the early Christians that God scattered them out away from Jerusalem (see Acts 8:1). In this case, God wanted them to spread out and preach the Gospel, which they did (Acts 8:4).

2. By Direct Control of One's Thought Life

If we study Proverbs 16:1, 9; 21:1 we see that it is clearly stated that God exercises a certain amount of direct control over men's thoughts and actions. He is able to cause a man's mind to have a certain thought just as He is able to do anything else He pleases, since He is omnipotent (see Rev. 17: 17).

Furthermore, in Philippians 2:13 Paul states that it is God who "worketh [literally, energizes] in you both to will [literally, to want to do] and to do [literally, to energetically do] of [that is, concerning] [His] good pleasure." It is on the basis of this verse that a Christian can have confidence that God will do His part toward communicating His will to us, provided we are fit recipients for His directions (see chap. 3). God can energize a man in such a way that he will develop a desire in his heart to want to do just what God wants. If God wants a man to go to England, for instance, the man may find himself experiencing a conscious desire to go to England.

To get that man to England God can energize him to go. God can energize him in such a way that he actually does those things that result in his going to England. Such is the way by which a Christian may be "led by the [Holy] Spirit" (Rom. 8:14; Gal. 5:18).

3. By Permitting Satan to Influence One's Thinking

The Bible clearly reveals that Satan, with God's permission, can influence our thinking. In Acts 5:4, Ananias is asked, "Why is it that you planned this deed in your heart?" Thus, Ananias thought it. In Acts 5:3 Peter asks Ananias, "Why did Satan fill your heart to deceive [by lies] the Holy Ghost?" So, Satan had something to do with the thought also.

The Bible doesn't reveal exactly what it is that Satan can do in influencing one's thoughts, so we can only speculate about it. I suspect that Satan tends to take a thought that is already in one's mind, perhaps a worry or fear, and in some way magnify it to where it tends to occupy the mind. He may make it stronger than it would be otherwise. He may make a problem seem worse than it really is. He may suggest something to the Christian that is not really true but which would worry one if it were true.

Satan does not speak to people in an audible voice. A phenomenon like this is usually considered a product of the imagination and may be a symptom of psychological disease.

If one has a thought that has been promoted by Satan, then it will seem just like any other ordinary thought. I don't know of any foolproof way to differentiate thoughts promoted in one's mind by Satan from thoughts that one would have inpendent of Satan's influence. There are some things to look for that should make one suspicious. Thoughts from Satan are always intended to lead us astray from God. They sometimes are for the purpose of making us doubt God. Sometimes they are for the purpose of influencing us to act rashly, independent of God's will. Regardless of whether the thought is from Satan or from us only, it is combated in a similar manner: by confronting it with the truth. Any unacceptable, untrue thought should be confronted with the truth.

I have mentioned Satan's activity at this point because this is another way in which God controls our thinking. Satan does nothing but what God permits. God permits nothing except that which fits in with His plan which He is carrying out. So, although Satan has an evil purpose in mind when he influences our thoughts, God has a good purpose in mind and still retains absolute control over the situation (see Job 1:12; 2:6).

C. THROUGH CONTROL OF CIRCUMSTANCES

I have mentioned previously that God may change circumstances in order to bring about a psychological effect on a person, and in this way maintain a form of indirect control over his thinking. The manipulation of circumstances may affect us in more ways than producing psychological effects. For instance, an outbreak of war in a certain place may result in a Christian soldier being moved about geographically to a different place, without affecting his thinking very much. We are all influenced by what happens in the world around us.

I thought it important to mention some of the Bible verses which clearly establish God's sovereignty (see Prov. 16:9; 20:24; 21:1; Acts 2:23; 4:28; Eph. 1:11). God does intervene in the affairs of men and bring to pass events and circumstances.

D. GOD NO LONGER USES DREAMS OR VISIONS

We do have Biblical examples in which God revealed His will to men in dreams (Gen. 20:3, 6; 31:11, 24; I Kings 3: 5; Matt. 2:12-13) and in visions (Gen. 15:1; Zech. 1:7-8; Acts 10:10-11). However, there are two major reasons why God does not use dreams or visions now as a way of revealing His will.

In the first place, after Christ's death and resurrection men did receive revelatory dreams and visions from God, but only up until the time when the writing of the New Testament was completed. In Acts 9:3 and 16:9-10 Paul had visions, but then Paul had not yet finished writing his inspired epistles, which make up a large part of the New Testament. After the visions to John the Apostle, recorded in the Book of Revelation, the visions ceased. In the New Testament God finished revealing all that He wants men to know. The Old Testament and the New Testament together constitute a complete record of the truth which God wanted revealed to men. Anyone who claims to have received any new truth by revelation through a dream or vision has the burden of proving his claim. In the days of the apostles, such as Paul and Peter, they were granted power from God to perform miraculous acts. They also received revelations of truth in dreams and visions. Such miracles supported their claims of being spokesmen for God. Thus, their message was established as authentic. This authenticated body of truth, recorded as the New Testament epistles, became the authoritative guide for Christians after the apostles passed off the scene. This body of truth, called "the faith" in Jude 3, has once for all been delivered to us.

The use of dreams and visions as a method of revealing truth properly belonged to the B.C. and apostolic (first 100 years A.D.) eras only. After the apostolic era passed, the need for dreams and visions also passed.

In the second place, since the advent of the Church Age, we have the unique leading ministry of God the Holy Spirit, who indwells the Christian and helps guide him. With the Holy Spirit energizing us and leading us, there is no longer any need for such dramatic methods as dreams or visions from God. Why should God use such a method when the Holy Spirit is adequate to communicate God's will to men? If God does still use dreams or visions today in communicating with Christians, then it must indeed be very rare.

This does not mean that we cannot acquire insight into ourselves and other things by studying our dreams. Frequently a dream is an expression, perhaps in disguised fashion, of the thoughts of our own mind. Sometimes a dream expresses an impression we gained on a subconscious level. It is very easy to claim that "God showed it to me in a dream," when in reality we simply learned something in a dream that was part of a natural learning process. Although God, since He regulates natural learning processes through natural laws, ultimately is the educator, yet this type of learning is not a miraculous revelation from God.

It is also true that God can remind us of something we learned from one of our dreams and use this fact in helping us to think our way clearly toward a decision that is His will for us. Yet, this thought would seem like any normal thought to us, not a special miracle.

What of people today who have had dreams of a seemingly supernatural nature? Some people have anticipated things in

the future or guessed the answer to problems that are difficult
to solve. These dreams are not easy to explain. Perhaps they
are related to that group of phenomena called extrasensory
perception. There is no doubt about the existence of extrasensory perception; this is being studied scientifically at one
university in this country. It seems to be regulated by laws
that are poorly understood. Yet, a dream foretelling the future still is not a revelation by God of His will for the future.
These phenomena are not limited to Christians, but are experienced by many unsaved people. In fact, I am informed
by a missionary friend that sometimes an unsaved person may
be guided to the Gospel and salvation partly as a result of
having some dream which obviously is unusual and perhaps
which foretells some future event, an extrasensory phenomenon.

The fact remains that God has no need of dreams or visions today to communicate His will to Christians. The
Bible and God the Holy Spirit are sufficient for this purpose.
Notice that I do not say that God cannot use dreams or visions, but that He does not do so today.

E. EVALUATION OF GOD'S METHODS

The mind is constantly receiving stimulation from visual,
auditory, or other impressions and memories, constantly re-
sponding to such stimulation with a steady flow of thoughts,
wishes, feelings, and emotions. This is the usual natural operation of the human mind. In addition, we can accept as
likely the presence, at times, of thoughts introduced by Satan
or by God.

But from the viewpoint of the person who is experiencing
all these thoughts and feelings, he is aware only of having

the thoughts. He has the problem of sorting out these thoughts and determining which are acceptable and desirable; which ones can be permitted expression in action; which ones must be denied gratification; which ones can be considered God's will for one's life. How to know? It is this question, how to know, which I have tried to answer in this book.

There are certain prerequisites which must be met before one can accurately know the will of God for his life. One prerequisite is that of accepting Christ as one's Saviour and thus becoming a Christian. This means that one must have a personal relationship with God by trusting in Jesus Christ. All that God says in the Bible about determining His will is directed to Christians only. Therefore, before going any farther a man should be certain that he has put his faith in Christ.

All the other prerequisites and some signposts essential to being successful in determining the Lord's will make up the major content of this book. In addition, I have devoted a special chapter to the common problem of so-called doubtful things. Certain principles are discussed which should be helpful in evaluating something of this nature. An attempt is also made to take up some common problems involved in deciding about God's will.

The way in which the Lord makes known His will is marvelous and accurate. It is the imperfect and incompetent human recipient of His will who tends to make mistakes. God's method is good, but the instrument through whom God is working is sometimes defective. The purpose of this study is to help reduce the frequency of the human mistakes.

Chapter 3

WHAT ARE THE PREREQUISITES FOR DETERMINING GOD'S WILL?

A. GOOD PHYSICAL CONDITION

BECAUSE THE MIND is housed in the brain and because the brain is a part of the physical body, anything which affects the body also affects the functioning of the mind.

For example, it is quite risky to try to make a decision about the Lord's will while one is deathly sick or fatigued and tired from lack of sleep. Here one is more likely to make a mistake, because at such times the brain is not working as efficiently as it usually is. Something like an acute, severe emotional upset has a similar disrupting effect.

It seems almost unnecessary to mention this. Yet we tend to forget this fact and make decisions when instead we should wait until we feel better.

B. EMOTIONAL MATURITY

I don't think anyone will question the fact that a child could not be expected to be able to discern the Lord's will as accurately as an adult. But many adults retain some childish or immature ways of thinking and acting. They are adults physically and chronologically but still somewhat childish in their emotions and thinking. This is called emotional immaturity. The difference between childish and adult ways of thinking is clearly referred to in the Bible (see I Cor. 13:11).

How does it come to pass that an adult would still think and act as a child? We have to trace the cause of immaturity back to what happened to that person in childhood. Assuming the child was normal when he was born, then we have to notice what kind of environment he grew up in. Every child tends to make mistakes in judgment and perhaps create for himself difficulties in childhood. For example, every child is born with a wish to have his own way and to have everything he wants. It is a disappointment to every child when he begins realizing that he can't have everything just the way he wants it. The environment, depending upon whether it is good or bad, tends to make it easier or harder for the child to become more mature. By environment I mean the home, the school, and other places where the child is subjected to the influence of other people. If the environment is good enough, then the child probably will be able to give up childish ways of thinking and take on more adult, civilized ways. If the environment is very bad, causing problems that are too difficult or too numerous for him to solve in a healthy way, the child probably will continue to struggle with these problems even after he is an adult physically. One could say that his emotional development was, in part, arrested.

If the problems weren't solved satisfactorily in childhood, the person continues to try to solve them as an adult. But, in adulthood, because the problems have usually been submerged into the subconscious mind, he may not consciously realize what he is doing. There are many thinking processes active in the subconscious mind, but we are not consciously aware of them. Many of the conscious thoughts and feelings we have are end results of such subconscious thinking.

Yet, these subconscious thought processes influence our conscious thinking and our behavior just as much as conscious thoughts. An old unsolved childhood problem is still being struggled with, but now on a subconscious level. As long as it remains in the subconscious mind, such a problem is out of reach of our conscious control. The best way to deal with it usually is to bring it up into the conscious mind. When one becomes consciously aware of the problem, then he can consciously struggle with it and solve it.

The problem frequently consists of two or more opposing wishes or needs which create a conflict within the person, with resulting tension and nervousness. For example, a child may have been deprived of adequate attention from his parents. In adulthood he still wants to get this parental, indulgent attention, yet now feels ashamed at wanting such a thing. He wants it, but he doesn't want to want it. He would enjoy it, but to get it would make him feel guilty. So he is in conflict about it.

It is easy to see that the persistence of childish ways of thinking and the conflicts associated with it (that is, emotional immaturity) will limit a person's ability to think and act in an intelligent, logical and controlled way. The immature person will tend to think and act in some ways just as he did as a child. Any conscious conclusion he comes to is strongly influenced by his subconscious thinking processes of which he is unaware. His subconscious conflicts may forcefully drive him in a compulsive manner to think and act in a stereotyped and inappropriate way. This limits his ability to logically think through a problem and make a decision. He may think he has discerned the Lord's will, when actually he has reasoned in a very stereotyped manner as dictated by his underlying emotional problems.

How does the person manage to stay consciously unaware of these subconscious problems? What keeps them in the subconscious mind? The use of defense mechanisms enables the conflict to remain subconscious. These are mental maneuvers which help a person to stay unaware of something he does not want to think about consciously. Many of these mental maneuvers are subconscious themselves, so that a person frequently is unaware that he is using a defense mechanism. Sometimes, in the process of spontaneous maturation, one may become aware of a subconscious conflict or thought, without help from another person. Frequently, however, this requires the help of a psychiatrist or another person who is a shrewd objective observer.

Although it is not my purpose to discuss these defense mechanisms in detail, let me illustrate how the existence of such subconscious conflicts and their corresponding defense mechanisms can lead one astray in his thinking and thus in determining the will of God.

1. *Problem of Prejudice or Bias*

It has long been recognized that a prejudice or bias is the result of subconscious thinking. A prejudice is a dislike or liking for something or somebody for which the person is unable to give a valid, rational, or logical reason. He doesn't consciously know the real reason for his preference. He may rationalize some reason or other, but this is not the real reason. Others may see through his rationalization when he cannot see it himself.

The true reason for the bias or prejudice is subconscious. For instance, the real reason a man may resent male teachers is because he resents his father. If this resentment toward his father is unacceptable to him and he doesn't want to be aware of it, then he must do something to keep from learning about it. So, he may displace this resentment onto the teacher (who reminds him of his father because both are authority figures), thus giving some expression to the resentful feelings without learning whom he really resents.

Thus, by these mechanisms of displacement and rationalization he keeps himself unaware of his resentment toward his father. But he ends up by having an unreasonable, irrational and unalterable resentment toward male teachers. One usually cannot rid himself of such a prejudice without bringing the whole problem up into his conscious mind where he can then realize whom he really resents and deal with it. Then the prejudice against male teachers would drop off. Instead, he would be consciously aware of resentment toward his father. But this would be a real feeling, not a prejudice, and there would be some logical reason for the resentment.

Now then, while having such an unresolved prejudice against male teachers, suppose God wanted a certain Christian to become a student in a school with male teachers. When God energizes this man with a desire to go to this school, the man is thrown into conflict. His underlying resentment gives rise to a desire to not go to that school. This desire to avoid male teachers, due to resentment, creates the need for a decision not to go to that school. The Christian will probably rationalize a number of reasons why he shouldn't go, but the real reason has to do with his subconscious resentment. Thus, he is unlikely to go. Also, he is unlikely to be consciously convinced that it is God's will for him to go.

Such a man truly does not have "power over himself." Such is the meaning of the word for self-control used in I Corinthians 9:25 and Titus 1:8. Such a man is resistant to either knowing or doing the Lord's will in this case because of a prejudice which stems from a subconscious problem.

Furthermore, a prejudice or bias can deceive us into thinking a certain action is God's will for us, when actually it is what we alone want. We may rationalize about it and label it God's will. In such a case, what is perceived as being God's will by that person really is what he (subconsciously) wants.

This problem of bias explains why good Bible students, who are accurate and logical in most of their understanding of Scripture, can go wide of the mark and be quite incorrect and illogical about one particular subject. It is possible for a Christian to hold to an irrational belief about some doctrine due to a subconscious bias.

2. *Problem of Forgetting*

As a result of subconscious conflict we may have a need to forget certain things. Usually, what we forget is in some way linked up with the conflict that we don't want to consciously think about. Therefore, these things must be "forgotten" or else they may remind us of the unpleasant conflict in the subconscious mind. For instance, if someone has a conflict over giving money away, he may repeatedly "forget" to bring sufficient money to church to make a contribution. Because the act of giving money away makes that person upset, due to a subconscious conflict, then he has a subconscious need to forget about bringing the money. In this way he avoids doing that which upsets him emotionally.

What if God reveals His will to us, but we constantly "forget" to do it? This may be due to a subconscious need to forget. We are thus rendered less effective in carrying out the Lord's will.

3. *Problem of Compulsive Behavior*

Sometimes one knows what the Lord wants him to do and he wants to obey, yet he finds himself compulsively, perhaps seemingly against his will, doing something else (see Rom. 7:19). Sometimes it seems as if the person is compelled by some inner force to do that which he consciously doesn't want to do. If there is a subconscious conflict giving rise to a need to perform that particular action, this need will sometimes exert more influence upon our behavior than a conscious wish to do something else. The result is that one finds himself doing that which he consciously doesn't want to do. Moreover, he doesn't know why he does it, because the real reason is subconscious. Such a person lacks power over himself.

One example of such a case is the alcoholic, a compulsive drinker. Usually he doesn't know why he drinks. Frequently he will make a strong conscious effort to avoid drinking. But when the subconscious conflict produces enough tension, the need to drink arises and his mind will become occupied with a conscious wish to begin drinking. This wish may be uncontrollable.

4. *Problem of Compulsive Thinking*

The same mechanism is responsible for compulsive thinking. Compulsive thinking is having thoughts that cannot be put out of the mind. Inappropriate, perhaps even undesirable thoughts continue to come into the mind, and the person cannot rid himself of them. An example of this is one man I knew who occasionally had the thought, "I hate God." He wished he never thought anything like this and became very upset whenever he thought it. In such a case there is a subconscious need which gives rise to the thoughts.

Sometimes the end result of the subconscious conflict will be compulsive thinking of illogical thoughts. For example, a person may inappropriately feel guilty over some trivial matter like eating a large lunch when there is no particular reason to care how big a lunch is eaten. The guilty feeling is not really related to the lunch, but is actually related to something else which the person is not consciously aware of, something in the subconscious mind.

Or a person may be convinced that he must give huge sums of money to the church. He has the conscious thought, "It is God's will." Yet he carries out this giving compulsively, sometimes when the money is not needed, sometimes shamefully neglecting other needy and worthy causes, sometimes even neglecting to pay his own bills and perhaps making his own family suffer deprivation. If God wanted one's giving to go that far, then one would expect that God would also provide the extra funds in some way to enable that person to still pay his own bills and provide for the needs of his own family. The Bible directs us to give according to how we have prospered (I Cor. 16:2). This means to give proportionately and appropriately, as a general rule, holding back enough for necessary expenses.

But a compulsive giver is not able to think logically or plan appropriately in his giving, because the giving serves some purpose stemming from a subconscious conflict. It may be that the person feels ashamed or guilty about some wish or memory, and the giving represents an attempt to magically atone for the supposed sin. I say "supposed" because sometimes the wish is really not sinful but the person perceives it as sinful, and out of ignorance becomes ashamed of it. Such a wish makes him feel that he is bad, and giving may compensate for this by making him feel that he is good. He compulsively has to give in order to try to prove to himself over and over again that he is actually not bad but good. God's will may not figure in the transaction at all.

Or take the case of doubting. Sometimes a person will doubt almost everything he does. After locking the door, he may have doubt about whether he locked it and must compulsively go back and check it to be sure, perhaps doing this several times. Or he may wonder if he turned the gas stove off or if he wrote a check correctly. Or he may make a decision, but then immediately doubt it, sometimes resulting in a reluctance to go ahead and take any action on a matter.

He may try to make a decision about the Lord's will for his life, only to promptly and repeatedly doubt his decision. He is never able to feel secure in any particular decision.

Such doubt stems from subconscious conflicts and prevents the person from thinking in a logical manner about his decisions. The subconscious conflict produces a tendency to think and act in a certain way. It is compulsive in that the person seems compelled to think and act that way, even though it may not be logical and he consciously may not want to.

The compulsive doubter frequently has a conscience that is far too strict. This problem may stem from too much criticism when he was a child. As a child, criticized too often, he came to fear decisions of any kind because of the risk of being criticized if he made a mistake. To make a mistake and experience criticism becomes so painful emotionally to him that he tries to avoid ever making the decision. So he doubts. His conscience reflects the overly critical attitudes of the persons in his childhood environment (usually parents, perhaps older brothers or sisters, teachers) and frequently tells him he is wrong when he is actually right. Such a person, in order to be happy, has to learn to ignore the extreme, illogical reproaches of his conscience.

Again, we have to say that such a person does not have power over himself. He is not in good control of his own thinking processes.

5. *Shifts in Emotional Maturity*

Although we have not looked at all the ways in which maturity can affect one's ability to discern God's will, yet these are enough to see that emotional maturity is quite important. We should keep on maturing for the rest of our lives. The more mature we become, the better able we are to discern the Lord's will. Maturation may cause a shift in our thinking about the Lord's will.

Someone may raise the question, "How can we ever be sure about the Lord's will unless we have become aware of and have properly solved all subconscious conflicts we may have in our mind?" To answer this question I will say several things. The existence of subconscious conflicts does render a person less efficient in discerning God's will. But this does not mean that he is 100 percent ineffective. In spite of his conflicts, he will still be able to be correct in a large portion of his decisions, and this is reason enough for always trying to make an accurate decision. Furthermore, by closing or opening doors as we try to take action, God is able to over-rule our mistakes and prevent us from taking a wrong step.

Yet we still will make some mistakes. Sometimes God permits us to make a mistake so that we will become aware of an emotional problem or prejudice to which we can then direct our attention with a view to correcting it. Furthermore, God does not expect perfection from us. He knows that we are dust (Ps. 103:14) and He prefers that the vessels through which He works be made of clay so that the glory may belong to Him (II Cor. 4:7). The fact that we are imperfect vessels does not make it impossible for God to use us. Moreover, in the ministry of the Holy Spirit in leading us (Gal. 5:16, 25) God has provided us with help in finding our place in the will of God. The Spirit helps us in our infirmities (literally, weaknesses) (Rom. 8:26).

The obvious solution to emotional immaturity is to become more mature. This can happen spontaneously when one becomes aware of a conflict that used to be buried in the subconscious. Indeed, Paul recommends that Christians try to judge (literally, discern) themselves (I Cor. 11:31). Yet, such a process is often difficult to carry on by oneself. It is easier to do with the help of a competent psychiatrist. Such a process of maturation can also occur as a result of testing (see Rom. 5:3; James 1:2-4).

Today, psychiatric help is sought not only by people with serious mental disorders but also by many people who are only emotionally immature in some way and who want help in growing up emotionally. These people may be seeking greater happiness, greater effectiveness at work, greater abil-

ity as a marital partner or parent, or some other worthy goal.
If an individual was experiencing some difficulty in living the
Christian life effectively or in discerning God's will for his
life due to an emotional problem, then this would be a legitimate reason to seek psychiatric help. For a spiritual goal such
as this, I believe it would be necessary for the psychiatrist to
either be a Christian himself or else be very sympathetic toward Christianity. For an emotional problem not involving
one's religious principles or spiritual values, any competent
psychiatrist might be able to help, since an emotional problem can be approached and resolved on a strictly psychological basis.

C. SPIRITUAL MATURITY

In Hebrews 5:13-14 a clear distinction is made between
spiritually immature Christians, referred to as "unskilful [lit-
erally, inexperienced] in the word [or, matter] of righteousness" (v. 13), and mature Christians who "by reason of use
[literally, because of practice] have their senses [that is, pow-
ers of perception] exercised to discern [literally, for distin-
guishing between] both good and evil" (v. 14). Here it is
emphasized that the man of full age [literally, the mature
one] is able to distinguish between good and evil, and thus is
more efficient at discerning what is the Lord's will.

The word here for maturity (translated in the A.V. as "of
full age") is *teleios,* which has the basic idea of complete-
ness. When applied to the concept of maturity it means "full-
grown" or "mature." This same word, *teleios,* is used by Paul
in Ephesians 4:13 where he says that one of the purposes of
the ministry gifts is that the Christian might become a "perfect man" (literally, a mature man), meaning spiritually

mature. In Ephesians 4:14 Paul goes on to say that the maturity is needed "in order that we may no longer be infants, tossed to and fro and whirled around in circles by every wind of teaching by the trickery of men, [this trickery being accomplished] by a cunning craftiness which has as its purpose the furthering of the scheming, deceitful system which is characterized by a wandering astray [from the truth]" (literal, expanded translation). In other words, we need to be spiritually mature to have the proper judgment and discernment so as to avoid being misled by a theological system of falsehood inspired by Satan. Satan would like us to be misled as to what is the Lord's will, and we will be misled unless we are spiritually mature.

This same idea is the subject of Paul's prayer for the Colossian Christians (Col. 1:9). Here he prays that they might be filled (that is, become complete or fully developed) with the full knowledge of His (God's) will in the realm of every (kind of) wisdom and discernment. The word for "fill" here is *plēroō*, to fill or to complete. The idea is that the Christian's mind is to be pervaded throughout by the knowledge of God's will.

But what exactly do I mean by spiritual maturity? By this I mean something similar to ordinary maturity: namely, a giving up of ways of thinking used before one became a Christian, and a taking on of more mature (that is, more proper as a Christian) ways of thinking and behaving. When one first becomes a Christian he has some wisdom, but part of this wisdom is the "wisdom of the world." By this term I refer to any philosophy which is contrary to the truth of God. Paul says that the "wisdom of this world is foolishness [literally, stupidity] from the viewpoint of God" (I Cor. 3:

19). To put it simply, we have to learn a new philosophy or way of thinking, which Paul calls "God's wisdom" (I Cor. 2:7). Paul says that there is a "wisdom we speak among the mature ones [again *teleios*]," but that it is not a wisdom known by the average non-Christian person in this age (I Cor. 2:6, 8). When our way of thinking has changed to where it closely corresponds to God's way of thinking, God's wisdom, then we are spiritually mature.

How do we acquire this new way of thinking? How is the old way of thinking dethroned? The Bible reveals several things about this process.

First, the learning of this new way of thinking is promoted by a teaching ministry of God the Holy Spirit. Christ said the Spirit would teach Christians when He came (John 16:13-14). John also emphasized that the Holy Spirit is really our teacher (I John 2:27), although He may utilize human instruments as tools for teaching, to whom He gives gifts of teaching ability (Eph. 4:11). The things taught by the Spirit (that is, God's wisdom) seem foolish to a non-Christian man because they can be understood only by the aid of the Holy Spirit (I Cor. 2:12-14).

Second, we come to really understand and use this new wisdom by applying it in our life experiences, especially in testing (Heb. 5:14; 12:7, 11). James urges us to count it all joy when we fall into testing (James 1:2). He adds that the aim of testing is to produce patience (patient endurance) (1:3). The resulting patience is to carry out its work in us in order that we may be mature (here *teleios* again) and intact, lacking in nothing (1:4).

The experience of testing demands that we put to use the new wisdom which we are learning, and in this way it be-

comes part of our permanent spiritual equipment. James
goes on to say that if any man lacks wisdom then he should
keep on praying to God who will give him the wisdom he
needs (James 1:5).

Paul, in Philippians 3:15, reminds us that mature ones
(*teleios*) are to be mature minded ("be thus minded" in
A.V.), and if anyone is thinking differently (that is, different from maturely or wisely), God will reveal this to him.
Here is God's promise that He will continue to make known
to us our immature ways of thinking.

So, by acquiring knowledge of the truth in God's Word
and by experiencing testing in which we get practice at applying the knowledge, we can become experienced and wise,
and thus mature.

That a man needs to be thinking along the lines of God's
wisdom is obvious if he is going to discern God's will (see
Isa. 55:8-9). To make a decision about a problem that is
close to what God wants one must think in much the same
way that God thinks. We need to be equipped with God's
wisdom in order to discern and do His will. (See Hebrews
13:21, where "make you perfect" is the A.V. translation of
the Greek word *katartizō,* to prepare or equip.)

It is not only mere knowledge that we must have, but a
strong and sincere conviction of the truth. It was only because of his strong conviction about the truth that Paul was
not ashamed of the Gospel and was therefore ready to go
about preaching it (Rom. 1:15-16; II Tim. 1:12). Because
Paul was not ashamed of the Gospel which he believed and
was willing to preach it, God was able to give him orders that
Paul would carry out.

Why would God issue an order to a Christian to go to a

certain geographical place to preach the Gospel, if that Christian so lacked conviction of the truth that he was afraid to speak of it? God may not waste effort giving orders where there is little or no possibility of their being carried out.

Until the Christian becomes mature and has acquired God's wisdom, there will remain a large portion of God's will that he cannot discern. The immature Christian is prone to being led astray into error, as Paul warns in I Timothy 3:6.

D. A PERMANENT DECISION OF YIELDEDNESS TO GOD'S WILL (Self-denial)

The central thought here is presented by Paul in Romans 12:1: "Therefore, I encourage you, brethren, by the mercies of God to present [literally, offer up for a sacrifice] your bodies a living sacrificial victim, holy, well-pleasing to God, which is your rational service" (literal, expanded translation). (See also Romans 6:13, 19.)

The central verb in Romans 12:1 is "present" or "offer up." This word was commonly used to refer to the act where the owner of the sacrificial victim (a lamb, perhaps) gives up (presents) his victim to the priest for use in the Jewish worship service.

Now, in the Christian era, Paul urges every Christian, as a believer-priest (I Peter 2:9; Rev. 1:6) to offer his entire person, including his body and mind, to God for the purpose of service. Once offered, God accepts, and from then on the person is obligated to perform whatever service or duty is asked by God. Also, from then on God is obligated to deal in a disciplinary manner with that person if he shirks his duty. Moreover, God is obligated to supply that person with directions and power for the carrying out of his duty. The context of the Book of Romans shows that the service in mind is that of living a proper Christian life, whatever this may involve. Such a life would include good works, adherence to a Biblical moral standard, use of gifts, preaching, or whatever special duties God may want carried out.

The sacrifice must be "living" because on earth only live people can be used for service. Dead people, in regard to earthly service, have lost their usefulness.

The person offering himself to God becomes "holy" in the sense that from then on he is set apart for service, much as an officer in the army is set apart for his particular duty.

This service is called rational (reasonable in A.V.). The literal meaning of this word is "that which pertains to the soul or reason." The idea is that it stems from the soul or mind or rational thinking faculties of the person. Thus, this once-for-all offering of oneself to God is a conscious, rational, deliberate act of presentation. The same thought is mentioned in Ephesians 6:6 in the phrase "doing the will of God from the soul."

The idea of this action is illustrated today by the act of a civilian man who enlists in the army. Before he enlists he is a citizen, sympathetic to the president, the commander-in-chief of the army. But he is not carrying out orders from the chief. In fact, he is receiving few, if any, orders. But after he enlists, everything changes. At the moment of enlistment he makes a conscious, rational, deliberate decision to serve in the army of the commander-in-chief. He takes an oath in which he swears to obey the chief's orders. From then on he does not have the same freedom he had before. He is obligated to go wherever the chief directs.

Just as the civilian does not have to enlist but does so because he wants to, likewise the Christian does not have to present himself to God for service. Paul, in Romans 12:1, does not command us to do this. Instead, he encourages or politely begs us to do so. But having once enlisted, one's status is not the same as before.

After enlistment, after presentation for service, whenever the soldier wants something that conflicts with what his chief wants, then the soldier must give up what he wants and obey his chief. This is what he has promised to do and this is what he is expected to do. Now, orders begin to come to him. It is the responsibility of the chief to get the orders to the new soldier, and it is the soldier's duty to carry them out.

If the soldier fails to carry out the order he faces the possibility of disciplinary action. The duty is important and cannot be taken lightly. To be useful a soldier must be obedient and faithful.

The soldier has to undergo training, directed by the chief and his assistants. The soldier is equipped and given opportunities to practice using his equipment. Sonner or later he is sent into battle for action against the enemy.

All of these things stem from the original decision to present oneself for service. A soldier enlists only once for each enlistment. The verb "present" in Romans 12:1 is in the aorist tense, which suggests that there is only one enlistment and that it is a once-for-all action, a life-long commitment to serve God.

This illustration of the soldier is used by Paul in II Timothy 2:4 where he mentions that the good soldier avoids undue entanglement in civilian business matters in order that "he may please Him [God] who enrolled him as a soldier."

This point illustrates one aspect of what a Christian does when he presents himself for service to God. He makes a decision to put God's will first in his life. Other matters, such as civilian business affairs, must be secondary. If one's duty as a soldier conflicts with a civilian activity, then one's duty comes first. To be a good soldier takes time, energy, and concentration, and one will be ineffective if he is distracted and preoccupied with other things. This was the point Christ made in His comment on the disciple who keeps looking back, that is, who is distracted by other things (Luke 9:61-62).

Paul reminds us that the life of a soldier involves suffering some hardship (II Tim. 2:3). This means that sometimes, in order to carry out the will of the Lord, we will have to give up something we want and perhaps tolerate something we don't want. This brings up the concept of self-denial.

This term is used by Christ in the Gospels where He refers to it as the first condition for discipleship (Matt. 16:24; Mark 8:34; Luke 9:23). By discipleship the Lord did not mean salvation but service. The idea of denying oneself is to quit putting one's own way first. When what you want conflicts with what God wants, you deny yourself and choose what God wants. This does not mean that Christians shouldn't enjoy things that God has given us to enjoy (I Tim. 6:17), provided the enjoyment of them does not interfere with the performance of our duties as Christians.

In the garden of Gethsemane Christ said to God the Father, ". . . However, not what I want but what You [want]" (literal translation of Mark 14:36). To give up something you want involves a hardship. The soldier, when he enlists, gives up a number of things he would enjoy in civilian life in order to serve his chief. He may have to endure physical discomfort and emotional frustration. Even so, sometimes he may also continue to enjoy many things while serving successfully at the same time. To serve does not mean that one cannot also enjoy. It does mean that from time to time, when a conflict arises, one must give up something he wants in order to carry out God's will for his life.

In another place in the Gospels Christ is approached by a scribe (Matt. 8:19) who says, "I will follow you wherever you go." Thus he is saying, "I am presenting myself to you for service." But when Christ answered him (Matt. 8:19-20; Luke 9:57-58) He cautioned the man to consider the cost. He reminds the man that service may involve hardship, such as no certain dwelling place. Christ urged this man to first think it over and consider the cost of such a decision and the resulting duty. Then, if he makes such a decision, he will be less likely to falter later and disobey orders as a result of lack of determination.

Why does a Christian have to present himself to God for service before he can be successful in knowing the will of God for his life? I think it is obvious that it is useless for God to issue orders to a Christian until that person has made a decision to carry out God's orders. Otherwise, there would be no interest in carrying out the orders. A civilian does not think of himself as being obligated to obey orders issued for soldiers. How can a Christian know what city God wants him to live in when he has never been interested in obeying God's directions? Since he has never told God he will obey, why should God bother to command?

If God does not issue the command, the Christian cannot know God's will. God wants every Christian to present himself for service. For every Christian God has a will that includes many things. But the successful carrying out of this will includes the presentation for service and the subsequent obedience of the Christian. In regard to the Christian who never presents himself to God for service, I suspect that many times he will find himself in doubt and confusion as to God's will for his life. His own will is ruling in his life and this determines his decisions.

Now I do not imply that God never directs any orders to Christians who have not presented themselves for service. He does. However, God cannot get through to such undedicated Christians as successfully as He can to those who have presented themselves for service and who are truly interested in living a life of obedience.

E. A SINCERE DESIRE TO KNOW GOD'S WILL

A sincere desire to know God's will comes as a result of the lifetime decision to present oneself for service and to obey God. We who have presented ourselves to God for service logically need to know His will daily for the rest of our lives. Where does God want me to go? What does He want me to do there? How does He want me to do it? How long does He want me to stay? What should I not do? All such questions become quite important.

The prerequisite of wanting to know is clearly stated by Christ in John 7:17: "If someone should want to be doing His will, then he shall know about the teaching, whether it is from God or whether I am speaking from Myself" (literal translation).

The context of this verse is a visit Christ made to Jerusalem for the Feast of Tabernacles (John 7:2). Midway during the feast Christ begins teaching (John 7:14). His teaching produces a reaction and a question. The Jews marvel (wonder, John 7:15) at His ability to teach and debate and use the Scriptures. They ask the question: "How is it that this One knows learning, yet He has never been schooled?" (literal translation, John 7:15). By "learning" they mean the Scriptures and other literature. Their problem is as follows: They knew that Christ has not attended the Jewish theological seminary and yet He seems to know a lot. They ask: "How can we know that what He says is true, and thus from God? How or where did He learn it? How do we know that these things aren't merely His own ideas?"

Christ answers these questions in John 7:16 by saying that He was schooled in the seminary of God the Father, the One who sent Him. Thus, He claims that what He teaches is the truth and has its origin with God.

Then Christ anticipates and answers their next question before it is asked: "How can we know that your teaching is from God the Father?" This is very close to the question a Christian has to ask himself and answer every day: "How do I know whether this decision stems from God or from my human mind?"

Christ gave them two ways to know. The second way He mentioned in John 7:18 when He pointed out that His ministry glorified God rather than Himself. Thus, the question is, "Whom does it glorify?" The first way He gave, in John 7:17, is what I wish to take up: "If someone wants to be doing His will, then he shall know. . . ." If one really wants to know and do God's will, the truth, then God will see to it that he learns the truth.

Now we have the principle: If a man wants to be doing

God's will, this is proof that he wants to know God's will, and God rewards his wish to know by seeing to it that he does learn God's will. Since there is a reasonable expectation of obedience, God reveals His will.

The principle can be stated in another way: If one uses the light (truth) that God gives him, then God will honor that obedience by giving his more light, that is, by revealing more of His will (Mark 4:24-25). Cornelius, a godly Gentile, was a man who lived up to the light he had. He feared God and was a righteous man (Acts 10:22). Peter, after Cornelius was saved and became a Christian, said that one who fears God and practices righteousness (that is, does the thing he knows to be right) is acceptable to God (Acts 10:35). Because Cornelius had used the light he had, God gave him more light, in this case the truth about salvation in Christ, and he was saved (Acts 10:44, 47).

God will keep on giving light as long as the Christian keeps on using it. However, according to the warning in I John 2:11, one who does not use the light he has (that is, chooses to walk in the darkness), eventually becomes blinded by the darkness. After that, he is unable to see the light (that is, he is unable to see or comprehend new truth). So, when we really want to know God's will for our lives and manifest obedience to His will, God faithfully continues to reveal His will to us.

F. A DAY-BY-DAY WILLINGNESS TO OBEY GOD'S WILL (Taking up the Cross)

As a result of our presentation to God for service we begin receiving orders from Him from day to day. As soldiers for

Christ, we want to obey our Commander-in-chief. We are motivated by God the Holy Spirit to do those things which constitute God's will for us. We also have the human nature, the flesh, which still longs to do what it wants. What the human nature wants to do and what God wants the Christian to do sometimes conflict (Rom. 7:23; Gal. 5:17). Sometimes a person finds himself feeling ambivalent about doing God's will. Half wants to obey, but the other half wants to do something different. It is because of this resistant half that one sometimes rationalizes about the decision and may carry out what is mistakenly called God's will, when really it is one's own will. Or, as a result of a divided determination, one may be unable to consciously decide about the matter, and thus ends up confused about what is the Lord's will.

Now this becomes a problem especially when the conflict is not thoroughly conscious and is instead pushed into the subconscious mind. Unless one realistically admits to himself the truth about his human resistance to obeying God's will, he cannot deal with it rationally or effectively. The subconscious part of the mind may fool one into believing a rationalization and thus allow the person to have his own way. This may happen without the person being consciously aware that he has fooled himself and has followed his own way instead of God's way. To deal with such a conflict successfully one has to make it conscious.

Just making it a conscious conflict instead of a subconscious one does not guarantee that one will make the right choice to obey God's will. But it does make it possible to use all of the self-control and determination available to try to make the right choice. One's willingness to obey the Lord varies from day to day and from moment to moment. Life contains a series of situations where one has to make choices between God's will and his own will.

A good example of this conflict is the reluctant disciple who, in response to Christ's command to follow (Luke 9:59), replies: "Let me first go and bury my father" (Luke 9:59; Matt. 8:21). To bury one's father was a sacred duty to the Jew. On the human level this man had a strong desire to continue living at home until the time of his father's death, then to bury him, and then to take up his duties in service to Christ. But Christ was calling him into active duty right then, that of announcing the good news about Christ (see Luke 9:60; Matt. 8:22). This threw the man into great conflict. He should put Christ first and not "me first" (notice the "me first" phrase twice in Luke 9:59 and 9:61). The choice he made depended upon the strength of his willingness on that day to obey Christ.

This matter of day-by-day conflict and choice is referred to by Christ as "taking up one's cross" (Matt. 16:24; Mark 8:34; Luke 9:23). At that time, the cross to the disciples was the carrying out of those commands and instructions of Christ, such as preaching, that would bring to them personal inconvenience, persecution and suffering from the hostile world-system. To us today the cross would refer to any command of God to us which would be unpleasant or which would be likely to bring trouble or suffering upon us. Perhaps every day there may be something we think of that we should do. Yet, because it may bring some unpleasantness, we sometimes balk at doing it. In Luke's Gospel account the word "daily" is part of Christ's command, thus emphasizing that the matter of making choices and taking up one's cross occurs from day to day (Luke 9:23).

So in this section I am referring to the Christian's day-by-day practice. The Bible states an important principle about our daily practice. Part of us wants to obey God; the other part wants to carry out our own will. Whichever part we keep on giving in to, day after day, it is to this part that we become a slave (Rom. 6:16; II Peter 2:19). By giving in to our sinful human wishes repeatedly over a long period of time we develop a habit of doing this. As a result of forming such a habit one reaches a condition where it is extremely difficult to deny oneself something that is wanted. Instead of being a willing slave to God, an obedient soldier, such a person is a slave to his own wishes.

However, before we were Christians this was the state of all of us. It was our nature, our habitual practice, to do our own will (Eph. 2:3; Col. 3:7). This habit of ours did not change immediately after salvation, but it did become possible for it to change. As a result of Christ's death, the enslaving power of the sin principle—the tendency to sin—was revoked, making it possible for one to choose to obey the principle of righteousness (that is, to choose to obey God's will) (see Rom. 6:6-7). Then it is up to the new Christian to consciously decide to stop repeatedly giving in to his sin tendency and instead to present himself to God for service (Rom. 6:12-14, 22). He presents himself for service only once. Then, after that initial presentation, he struggles daily in conflict, perhaps being pulled in two directions: one, God's way; the other, his own way. If one wants to carry out God's will, he can.

But everyone fails from time to time in his daily practice.

Why? Because the flesh is weak (Rom. 6:19; 7:18; Matt. 26:41). Our normal human tendencies keep on asserting themselves. God helps us to get the victory over this habit of having one's own way by a gradual process of retraining. To get to the point where one forms the new habit of denying his own way whenever it conflicts with God's way takes time and practice. (See II Corinthians 10:5: "taking captive every thought as a prisoner for the obedience to Christ" —a literal, expanded translation.) Therefore, one of the prerequisites which helps us in being highly successful in discerning the Lord's will is experience. How God works with us in this process is discussed at more length in the section on experience.

Remember that the central point of this section is that we must be willing to obey God's will. This willingness must be maintained day by day for success in discerning God's will.

G. WILLINGNESS TO ACCEPT THE AUTHORITY OF THE WORD OF GOD ("Follow Me")

Since God has revealed a large portion of His will in the Bible, it logically follows that unless one accepts the Bible as an authoritative guide, as truly the Word of God, he cannot know or accept God's will as the Bible reveals it.

This is a crucial problem to a Christian who has doubts about the integrity and authority of the Scriptures. Such a person is in doubt about what God expects of him, since he cannot allow himself to be guided by the Bible. Most genuine Christians do not doubt that the Bible is really the Word of God.

There is a more common problem with the average Christian: namely, an unwillingness to admit that a particular area of his life is not as it should be. He may be aware of Bible instruction that refers to this area of his life, but he has never done anything about it. He wants to hang onto the sin in that area of his life. He may readily obey Biblical commands regarding other areas of his life, yet be very resistant to changing in this one area.

For instance, a successful businessman may be quite willing to bring his life into conformity with the Word of God in such areas as his home life, his social life, his sex life, and his church life. Yet he may carefully avoid bringing Christian principles into his business life. He prefers to keep on doing business in the same way, perhaps using improper or dishonest business practices. Perhaps he doesn't want to change his business methods for fear of loss of income, business failure or criticism. These fears may cause him to resist the changes that the Word of God suggests. Thus, comparing his life to a house and the Word of God to a visitor, he has welcomed his visiting guest into every room in his house except one. Into this room he will not let the visitor go. The guest is not welcome there.

This is the concept Paul used in Colossians 3:16 when he said: "As for the Word of Christ, let it habitually be at home in you abundantly" (a literal, expanded translation). The idea of the verb translated "dwell" in the A.V. is "to be at home." It was used to refer to the place where a person made his permanent home and had free run of the house. A person might stay temporarily at many places, but only when he arrived at his permanent residence could he say he was "at home."

So Paul is urging Christians to let the Word of God "be at home" in them abundantly. By this he meant: accept the

Word of God as the authoritative standard to which you should conform your life and apply that standard to every area of your life. In other words, let the guest have free access to every room in the house as a permanent resident of the house. This is seen in the word "abundantly." Every area of our life is to be brought into conformity with the Word of God.

If one is unwilling to do this he may deliberately remain ignorant of or (subconsciously) may not understand what the Bible says about a particular issue in his life. In such a case how can he possibly know the Lord's will regarding that issue?

For example, I have seen godly women who devoted much time and effort to spreading the Gospel, teaching the Bible, helping the saints, and pursuing other worthy activities. Yet, in spite of their constant Bible study, they never seemed to notice that the Bible says that the wives are to be workers at home ("keepers at home" in A.V.) (Titus 2:5), managing the household ("guide the house" in A.V.) (I Tim. 5:14), taking the time and energy and devotion it requires to love their husbands and their children (Titus 2:4). These are also good spiritual activities. The result of such neglect is a home that is not managed properly, a husband who is not loved sufficiently and is thus dissatisfied and resentful, and children who are deprived of the affection they need. It is difficult for a wife to be affectionate to her husband and display pure Christian behavior to him (I Peter 3:2) if she is seldom at home with him.

Now I do not intend to suggest that wives should stay at home all the time. They should have some satisfying and recreational activities outside the home. It is a matter of having the proper balance. Husbands may resent Christian activities because they seem to have taken their wives away from them. It is possible that an unsaved husband may tend to react with hostility to Christianity for such a reason. But how could he be expected to react otherwise when he is neglected by his wife who fails to give him the attention and affection that he deserves as her husband? In such a case part of the blame for the husband's attitude must be put upon the wife, who refuses to recognize her responsibilities to her own husband within her marriage. She has failed to let the Biblical standard influence her treatment of her husband.

Or, take the example of the devoted pastor who relentlessly drives himself in his pastoral ministry to the flock, only to neglect his equally important ministry to his own wife and children at home. He is careful to be a good pastor but fails to invest the necessary time and energy required to be a successful husband and father.

This principle of willingness to accept the authority of the Word of God is given by Christ as the third prerequisite for being a disciple, and He phrased it as follows: "Keep on following Me" (Matt. 16:24; Mark 8:34; Luke 9:23). He meant us to follow Him in obedience to His example and His word, to walk the road of obedience. Christ does not pretend that such a road of obedience isn't "narrow" (Matt. 7:14). It is narrow, hedged in by many dos and don'ts. But staying on that road makes possible effective service to God, which will bring rewards in Heaven.

So don't lock up any rooms in your life. Don't try to keep God out of any area of your life. Apply the standard of God's Word to every part of your everyday practice.

H. WILLINGNESS TO USE THE "BY FAITH THROUGH THE SPIRIT" METHOD

I have mentioned previously that much of the responsibility for getting the will of God across to the Christian rests with God Himself. How does the Lord accomplish this?

God communicates His will to one's mind through the Holy Spirit. This ministry of leading by the Spirit is referred to in the Bible as being "led by the Spirit" (Rom. 8:14; Gal. 5:18). Examples of this ministry by the Spirit are found in Acts 8:29; 11:12; 16:7.

In Galatians 5:17 it is stated that the Holy Spirit competes with one's own will (the flesh) for mastery over the person and for control over the choice that is made. Everyone naturally wants to have his own way. Paul says that when one walks by the Spirit he will not fulfill the lust of the flesh (Gal. 5:16). (Notice, this statement does not promise sinless perfection but rather freedom from slavery to sin.) The word "by" ("in" A.V.) is added in the translation to communicate the idea of the Greek dative case. It may refer to sphere (that is, "walk in [the sphere of] the Spirit"); this would mean to behave within the limits marked off by the Spirit. The word "by" may also mean "by means of" or "in dependence upon." When one goes the way the Spirit leads, he is manifesting in this obedience his dependence upon the Spirit for proper guidance. The heart attitude of trust is manifested by the outward act of going where the Spirit leads. So Paul urges Christians to "keep on following in line with the Spirit" (literal expanded translation of Gal. 5:25), the idea being to behave and go as the Spirit directs.

Now on the human conscious level one is not aware of

any unique sensation or feeling that can be distinguished as exclusively the leading of the Spirit. Thoughts that come to one's mind as a result of the Spirit's ministry of leading seem just like any other thoughts that enter the mind. How can one tell the difference? How does one know when the thought or wish has been implanted there by God, and when it stems from one's own will?

The answer is that there isn't any scientific way to test it and thus know. Therefore, the Christian must rely upon the "by faith" method (II Cor. 5:7; Heb. 11:17, 27). The entire Christian walk is to be by faith, and this includes also that part of the walk which has to do with discerning the Lord's will. By faith we believe that God will see to it that we have the correct wish and that we will carry out the correct wish that will accurately accomplish His will (Phil. 2:13). This method was known to Old Testament saints (see Ps. 37:5; Prov. 3:5-6). But is there a New Testament verse which clearly promises such an operation by God? The answer is "Yes."

The best verse to show forth this fact is Philippians 2:13: "For God is the One who is energizing you both to want to do and effectively do on behalf of [His] good pleasure" (literal, expanded translation). In this verse Paul says that God energizes Christians. The word "energize" (translated "worketh" in the A. V.) is the word *energeō,* from which we get our word "energy." It refers to the concept of operative power. The meaning is to energize, or to work effectively, to produce an effect, to produce some effect in someone. God, using His power, produces in us a desire to "want to do" that which is His will. He energizes us to have a conscious wish that fits in with what pleases Him. He also energizes us in such a way that we carry out and perform that which He wants us to do. He infuses us with the energy and power to carry out the wish he has implanted (Col. 1:29).

So, by faith the Christian has to trust that what he finds himself wanting to do is exactly what God wants him to do.

But someone will immediately object that by doing what he wants to do, he might carry out his own will instead of God's will. Now this particular fear is the reason why the Christian must proceed "by faith." How does anyone ever become absolutely certain that his conscious wish is not his own way instead of God's way? There is no way to do so, except to trust that God will energize one to want to do and to do that which God wants; that He will open or shut doors to keep one on the right track; that He will keep one from getting on the wrong road; or that He will tell one when he gets on the wrong road. It is God's responsibility to either block a person from making a wrong choice or tell him when he has made a mistake. If we, by faith, trust in Him to do His part, and if we fulfill to our best ability the prerequisites and follow the signposts, He will not let us down.

The Christian should not become so preoccupied with what he should or shouldn't do that he forgets to notice what God is energizing him to want to do. God will cause us to want to do the proper thing. It is because of this fact and the provision of God's power that the Apostle John can say that the commandments of God are not grievous (that is, difficult to obey) (I John 5:3).

This does not mean that Christians will never make mistakes regarding the Lord's will. Along with the conscious desire to do what God wants there usually exists also the conscious desire to do that which stems from one's own will.

We all make mistakes. We are human, therefore we are defective instruments. God's method of communicating His will is good, but the human instrument is not completely reliable. No one will be perfect or complete in fulfilling the prerequisites or in following the signposts. The human tendency to go one's own way instead of the way of obedience will remain until death. This tendency leads to mistaken decisions about the Lord's will. We tend to forget things we need to remember. We are lazy about learning the Word of God, which is necessary for proper leading by God. God can make a Christian realize that he is following a wrong path, forbidden by the Bible. But this realization is more difficult to accomplish when the Christian does not know the Bible. If the Christian is strongly motivated by subconscious conflicts so that what he consciously wants to do is determined by his subconscious emotional needs, then certainly he will make mistakes. While embroiled in emotional conflict he really is not mentally free to choose the Lord's will. His subconscious emotional needs tend to fool him into choosing that which attempts to satisfy or solve the subconscious problem.

Nevertheless, we must go on and try to make decisions concerning God's will, trusting that God will either guide us correctly or reveal to us when we have made a mistake. The "by faith" method is the only reliable way. Adherence to this method will help avoid the amazing rigidity sometimes manifested by certain Christians. These people, relying upon other methods, frequently come up with a list of dos and don'ts which they think is infallible and which they think should be binding upon everyone. Such people find it hard to change their convictions when necessary, and thus fail to benefit from new insight which the Lord could give them if they were not so rigid and dogmatic.

I. WILLINGNESS TO PRAY AND WAIT FOR GOD'S WILL TO BECOME KNOWN

James recommends that when the Christian lacks wisdom he should "keep on asking" (for it) from God, who gives to all generously and does not reproach, and it shall be given to him (James 1:5). James uses the present tense in this verse, properly translated as "keep on asking," because sometimes the answer does not come immediately. When it doesn't come right away, the Christian should keep on praying, and wait for it.

But when one does not get an answer immediately, he tends to doubt. So James cautions the Christian not to doubt (James 1:6) but to keep on asking in faith.

Why would God make us wait for the answer? In the first place, God is not our servant whose only interest is to get whatever we want. He doesn't have to jump when we speak. When the time comes that we truly need to have the answer and know His will, He will see to it that we know it.

In the second place, we may not be asking the right question of God (see Rom. 8:26). God may want to deal with us about what we are asking, trying to help us perceive our problems more clearly and thus ask more intelligently.

So we have to be patient (Ps. 37:7). As we continue to struggle toward reaching a decision, we can be sure that God is doing His part toward helping us think correctly about the problem.

J. EXPERIENCE

At the end of section F I pointed out that experience in discerning the Lord's will is necessary because of the need for retraining us in denying our own way when necessary and choosing God's way. As I said before, the Christian brings with him his past habits, including that of habitually doing anything he wants to do (Eph. 2:3; Col. 3:7). Although he may desire to change immediately to a state in which he behaves mostly by new spiritual habits, the fact is that usually this does not happen. The habits of a lifetime are not that easily uprooted. Some habits may leave immediately after salvation, but usually many will remain. These unspiritual habits should be regarded as undesirable by the new Christian, who then begins struggling to throw off these old ways of behavior. What method does God use in helping us uproot these undesirable habits?

God's method is suffering. If one responds properly to the experience of suffering in a trial or test, he will find that the experience helps to overcome the power of previously established undesirable habits. Peter said that "he who has suffered in the flesh has ceased from [the enslaving habits of] sin, to the end that he might pass the remaining period of his life while in the body no longer [in slavery] to the lusts of men but rather [in submission] to the will of God" (literal expanded translation of I Peter 4:1-2). There is no doubt that suffering causes a weakening of our personality habits. Such weakening then makes it possible for them to change for the good.

Suffering also makes it necessary for us to exercise our faith, thus giving us an opportunity to get practice in using new spiritual habits of thinking and behavior. It is practice that enables us to become competent in discerning the Lord's will (Heb. 5:14). Christ, because He was truly human, also had to become competent in obedience by the route of suffering (Heb. 5:8).

After the trial has served its purpose then God relieves the suffering. If we have been damaged in an undesirable way spiritually, God repairs the damage (I Peter 5:10). In this verse the word translated "make you perfect" in the A.V. means to "repair" and is used of mending nets in Mark 1:19.

We need to have a proper attitude toward suffering in order to benefit from it. At the time it is not enjoyable (I Peter 1:6), but if we are properly exercised by it then we will reap great profit from it (Heb. 12:11). Peter emphasizes the necessity of the right attitude when he tells us, "Arm yourselves with the same mind" (that is, way of thinking) (I Peter 4:1). What way of thinking does he refer to? Here he is talking about the same attitude toward suffering that Christ had. He is referring to the fact that was proved by Christ's example. The fact is that suffering is invariably followed by blessing. Christ suffered greatly but afterward was blessed and highly exalted by God. God does not permit a Christian to suffer unless it is for the purpose of helping him in some way (Rom. 8:28).

Having such an attitude as this toward suffering makes it bearable. Looking forward to the blessing, we can suffer through the trial.

So the process of uprooting one's old undesirable habits of behavior is a gradual one that goes on all of our earthly life, involving repeated testing which is followed by blessing. It is this process that Paul had in mind in Romans 12:2: "Stop being conformed to the pattern of this age, but rather be becoming transfigured by the renewing of your mind, so that you may prove [by a process of testing] what [is] the will of God, which [will is] good and well-pleasing and complete" (literal, expanded translation). Peter also refers to it in I Peter 1:14: "Inasmuch as [you are] children of obedience, no longer conforming yourselves according to the pattern of your former lusts at the time of your ignorance" (literal translation).

An older Christian with much experience should be more skillful at discerning the Lord's will. It takes experience. This is one reason why Paul instructs Timothy not to appoint a recent convert to the office of elder (I Tim. 3:6).

Chapter 4

WHAT ARE THE SIGNPOSTS IN DETERMINING GOD'S WILL?

HAVING TRIED to satisfy the prerequisites mentioned in the previous chapter, one is now ready to make a formal approach to a decision about the Lord's will. If one has not adequately fulfilled all the prerequisites, his final decision may sometimes be erroneous. However, none of us is perfect. All that anyone can do is make the most effective use he can of his abilities and then aim at improvement in his weak areas.

In approaching a decision about God's will I think it is helpful to make a checklist of signposts by which one can be guided. This is similar to the pilot who gets his landmarks lined up properly and who goes over his checklists so as to land his plane safely and in the correct place . .

A. GOD'S WILL AS ALREADY REVEALED IN THE BIBLE

This is the first and most obvious signpost. David said, "Thy word is a lamp unto my feet, and a light unto my path" (Ps. 119:105). An example of such guidance is the clear instruction in the Bible that a Christian is to marry only another Christian (I Cor. 7:39; II Cor. 6:14). In considering whom to marry, a Christian should consider this point as binding, in the sense that the marriage should not be carried out unless this condition is met. Thus, we can say that it is never God's will for a Christian to marry someone who is not a Christian.

God the Holy Spirit uses the Word of God in leading us. When the Spirit is energizing one to think about a decision that must be made, He frequently uses one's knowledge of the Scriptures and reminds one of a verse which helps to decide that particular issue.

Now the Bible, to be used properly, must be approached properly. Many Christians misuse the Bible and make improper interpretations and applications. They may actually be led astray in their Christian behavior by an improper application of a Biblical truth. Thus it is necessary to discuss the proper use of the Bible.

First, it is important to use a good translation. The Bible originally was not written in English. The Old Testament was written in Hebrew, with a few parts in Aramaic. The New Testament was originally written in Greek. Both must be translated into English before they can mean anything to us. Many people still use the King James Version, published in A.D. 1611. However, some of its words are obsolete or have changed in meaning. In many places the King James translation does not fully convey what the author was really saying. Why should Christians be bound to this translation when more accurate ones are available?

Several more recent translations which are good are: (1) American Standard Version, published in 1901; (2) Berkeley Version; and (3) a New Translation of the Bible by J. N. Darby. If one wants to concentrate upon the New

Testament, there are several that are very good: (1) Williams' translation of the New Testament; (2) the Amplified New Testament; and (3) Kenneth Wuest's expanded translation of the New Testament. My vote for the best and most useful of these goes to the New Testament translation by Wuest. Obviously we must know, as accurately as possible, exactly what God has said in the Bible before we can determine what He meant by what He said. This requires a good translation.

Second, one must use a method of interpretation that acknowledges the fact of the inspiration of the Scriptures (II Tim. 3:16) but does not ignore such important things as historical background. I believe the only justifiable and accurate method of interpretation is that known as the grammatical-historical method.

This method assumes that each word in the Bible is used to convey the ordinary, customary meaning which it conveyed in that language at the time that particular book was written. Thus, this method involves studying not only the word itself and its possible meanings, but also the cultural and historical background in which the word was used. For instance, a marriage ceremony means one thing to us today in America, but in the first century A.D. it involved entirely different cultural procedures within the Roman empire, especially in the Jewish culture. An average Christian, studying the Bible, could learn a lot of this historical background by buying a good Bible dictionary or encyclopedia. As to the real meanings of the word, this should be explained in the translation, either by a footnote on the page giving a fuller explanation of the word or by expanding the translation in such a way as to get across the meaning (as Wuest has done in his translation).

This method recommends that any interpretation be based upon sound grammatical evidence derived from the actual Biblical text. It insists that doctrine be based upon what the Bible actually says and not upon what some church creed pronounces. It insists that the rules of grammatical construction be followed in determining what a particular sentence says and means. It considers the context of the section before determining the meaning of a verse in that section. It considers the over-all plan or argument of that particular book before trying to determine the meaning of the many parts of the book.

To use any method other than this means that one has to either rely upon the opinion of someone else, who may be wrong, or guess at what the interpretation is, relying upon one's own opinion. When one begins using such "opinions" the resulting interpretations frequently reflect a person's own preconceived ideas or prejudices. If one doesn't curb his imagination by the grammatical-historical method, he stands in danger of producing practically any interpretation of any verse he wishes.

Third, one must make a proper application of the verse. I don't think a person should make the mistake of thinking all of God's commands in the Bible are for him. Some are directed to other people, living in a different age. For instance, the Jews, living in the pre-Christ era, were directed to offer blood sacrifices in their worship. But this command was never intended to be a general command for all peoples in every age.

Yet some Christians today still become confused and try

to take the commandments of the Jewish law (Exod., chaps.
20—31), which are addressed clearly to Jews (Exod. 19:3;
31:13), and act as if they were directed to them. The Christian should realize that the rules which God intended to apply to Christians today in the Church Age are found in the
New Testament from Romans through Revelation. What
about the Gospels and the Book of Acts? They are books
which serve a specific purpose in covering the life and death
and resurrection of Christ, and also describe the transition
period between Judaism and Christianity. They must be interpreted and applied accordingly and appropriately. Some
things in the Gospels and Acts apply to Christians, and some
things apply only to the Jews. This does not mean that the
Old Testament has no value for Christians. There are many
historical facts in it which illustrate and confirm New Testament principles (see I Cor. 10:6, 11). There are many useful lessons that can be learned about God's dealings with
men.

My argument here is that the only proper application of a
Scripture verse must be based upon an intelligent interpretation of that verse which considers: (1) the historical and cultural situation in which the book was written and (2) to
whom the verse was addressed. So the Bible, properly translated, interpreted, and applied, is indeed a valuable signpost
in discerning the Lord's will.

B. WHAT DO I WANT TO DO?

This is an obvious signpost, if the Christian is trusting in
God to energize him to want to do that which God wants him
to do (see Phil. 2:13).

If one trusts in God to guide him and, perhaps by mistaken convictions, tries to proceed in a direction contrary to God's will, God can be relied upon to close the door: that is, to block the way. Sometimes, although the right course of action has not been decided upon and the Christian is unsure about it, circumstances may force him to make some sort of move, to do something. As long as a Christian is moving, trying to find the proper way, the Lord can actively guide him, opening a door here, perhaps closing a door there, until he arrives in the proper place (see Ps. 37:5).

We must not be so concerned with figuring out what we should do that we neglect noticing what we want to do.

C. THE CONSCIENCE

When one is considering doing something which violates some known scriptural principle or some basic moral value, his mind warns him against doing it. That part of the mind that says, "Don't do it; it's wrong," is the conscience.

I used the term "known scriptural principle" because to a certain extent the conscience is limited to one's knowledge of the truth. There are certain sins, such as murder or incest, which seem to be inherently known to be morally wrong. But many other wrongs must be learned. The conscience, being a function of the mind, is not always right. It is sometimes weak (I Cor. 8:7), meaning that it does not always have the right information and needs to be reeducated.

This education of the conscience is important. It is accomplished by acquiring a knowledge of the Bible. Paul, in I Timothy 1:19, indicates that some, by not maintaining a good conscience, fell into error and ended up in spiritual shipwreck.

Also, the conscience should be primarily toward God (Acts 24:16) and not just to men. Men do not always see what we do, but God does. Men tend to feel less restrained when other people cannot see them, forgetting that God still sees them. We need to remind ourselves that God and the angels (I Cor. 4:9; 11:10) are our spectators.

Furthermore, there is a danger in trying too hard to please men by not offending their consciences. The danger is that one may become a prisoner to the illogical and irrational prejudices of other people. To become enslaved to the opinions of others in this way makes it difficult for one's mind to be free to reason in a rational and logical way. A Christian trying to make a decision about God's will for his life must reason logically about it, using all the facts he has. He must be able to think for himself, thinking intelligently. To be bound to what others think makes him a slave to others. Such a person cannot be a servant (literally, bond-slave) of Christ (Gal. 1:10). Our first responsibility is to God, even though men may be offended by an act of obedience to God. Paul warns us against being misled by the judgments of other men (Col. 2:16-18).

A frequent psychological problem is that of the person with an overly strict conscience. This type of conscience comes about as a result of too much environmental criticism during childhood. Perhaps as a child one was unable to please his parents. Perhaps they found fault with most everything he did. Later, as an adult, he finds himself doubting that he can do anything right. He is still afraid that he will be criticized for what he does, so he is afraid to do anything. Every decision he makes is followed by doubts as to whether it is right. As a Christian such a person lacks confidence in many of the decisions he makes about the Lord's will, in spite of the fact that they may have been right decisions. It is a serious problem for him.

What can be done about this particular problem? He can get competent psychiatric treatment which may help to make his conscience less strict. Actually, he needs to learn to pay less attention to the overly strict, illogical part of his conscience. A true warning from God through the conscience is neither illogical nor irrational. If he is trusting in God to energize him to want the Lord's will, he can act in this direction and try to train himself to ignore the irrational doubts that stem from such an abnormal conscience.

Another psychiatric problem is that in which the conscience is not developed enough. This problem can also be treated psychiatrically. An underdeveloped conscience also stems from childhood problems, especially from an environment where the child never really had a close, loving relationship with someone who really accepted him as a person. The fear of displeasing someone who loves you and who is loved by you is a normal and important factor in developing a good healthy conscience. If there is no one who really loves the child, he feels he will lose nothing by his misbehavior and thus fails to develop sufficient self-control to keep from doing that which is wrong. Discipline is necessary for a child, but it must be preceded by and combined with love.

An underdeveloped conscience can also result from parental discipline which is too loose. A parent who is too easy on his child and lets him have his way too much is really not helping him. It is necessary to set reasonable limits upon a child's behavior.

The Christian with an overly strict conscience hangs back,

unsure of himself. He is doubtful and reluctant to go ahead with a decision about the Lord's will. The Christian with an underdeveloped conscience rushes ahead impulsively without enough forethought and makes decisions too quickly, often rashly and incorrectly.

The desirable balance is somewhere between these two extremes. One extreme is to wait forever for the Lord to reveal His will, when one would only have to go ahead in some direction and the Lord's will would quickly become obvious. A moving car can be guided more easily than a parked car. The other extreme is to jump into something too quickly, without taking sufficient time to consider all the important factors concerned.

One rule that should be noted in evaluating what the conscience says is: when the conscience is correct, it will always be based clearly upon some moral principle or some scriptural principle. One can always point to some verse in the Bible which legitimately supports the claim of the conscience. However, if the conscience says, "It's wrong, but I can't tell you why," and there never does emerge any rational reason why it would be wrong, one should suspect that the conclusion of the conscience was based on a prejudice or that the conscience is overly strict. If it is God warning you against a decision, He usually uses the truth of the Word of God. A vague, inappropriate, irrational doubt is frequently not from God but from one's own overly strict or misinformed conscience.

It is true that "whatsoever is not of faith is sin" (Rom. 14: 23). But to have an irrational doubt about something does not mean that it is "not of faith." The irrational doubt must be recognized for what it is—a symptom of a psychological problem—that of an overly strict conscience.

So, one must consider what the conscience says, but it should not have life or death veto power over a decision.

D. THE ADVICE OF YOUR PASTOR AND CHRISTIAN FRIENDS

Because you as a Christian may not know everything the Bible teaches and because your pastor or Christian friend probably knows some things that you do not, it is very helpful to consider the advice of such persons. I do not recommend that someone else make the decision for you, for that is your own responsibility. But you should consider their advice and try to profit from their experience. Sometimes they will point out something that you would never have thought of. A pastor usually has the advantage of years of experience in observing people as they try to discern the Lord's will, and he acquires a certain amount of wisdom in this area.

However, he is hedged in by the same limitations that every person has. He is not infallible and therefore should not be too dogmatic. Pastors should only be guides or leaders, ones to be imitated (Heb. 13:7); not rigid, authoritarian masters, lording it over their subjects (I Peter 5:3).

Any such advice from pastor or friend should always be measured by the standard of the Word of God.

E. COMMON SENSE

One would think it unnecessary to mention this signpost, but it is frequently neglected. The Lord expects us to use common sense and commands us to do so in the Bible. In Titus 2:12 we are commanded to "live soberly and righteous-

ly and godly in the present age." The word "soberly" is the
adverb form of the adjective *sōphrōn,* which means "sound-
minded." This adjective is found in I Timothy 3:2 and Titus
2:2, 5 and is translated as "sober" or "discreet." The real idea
of the word is about the same as our term "common sense"
used today in this country. It means to be "sensible." To fail
to be "sound-minded" or "sensible" is to be foolish.

By common sense I mean all truth about people and the
world and life in general that is useful to us in conducting
our affairs in daily life. It includes practical financial wisdom,
some basic knowledge of rules of good health, both physical
and psychological, and similar things. There is much useful
truth that is not written in the Bible. For example, the Bible
is not a textbook of science. Yet there is much useful information about health that has been discovered by medical science that we should put to use in our life. To ignore such
information and fail to put it to use is "foolish."

Suppose a missionary today is equipping himself for the
mission field and is buying a used car for use in his work. It
would be only common sense for him to have a good me-
chanic thoroughly check the car before he buys it. Otherwise,
he might waste the Lord's money on a car that would break
down quickly and be worthless to him.

Being led by the Spirit does not mean that we are to ignore
common sense but rather that we should utilize all the information available and try to make the most sensible decision possible.

However, it is also true that one should not follow the
course dictated by common sense so rigidly that the Holy
Spirit cannot possibly lead in a different direction. There are
times when the Spirit may lead a Christian to ignore a com-

mon sense principle and make a decision contrary to it. But this requires a definite, special leading by the Spirit, who does not usually lead one to ignore common sense.

I can recall an instance of a Christian businessman who was burdened about the financial needs of a Christian school. He knew little of the school's actual financial situation. In reality, the school was in danger of being closed down in foreclosure proceedings; so the need was urgent. This businessman was led by God to borrow a very large sum of money on his business to send to the school. The amount of money was so large that it was definitely contrary to sound business procedure, something common sense would strongly forbid. He was advised by good friends that his action was foolish, and ordinarily their advice would have been sound. Yet, he gave the money to the school, thus avoiding the foreclosure of the institution. His business later prospered and the Lord blessed him richly for his generous giving.

So in that case he had to ignore common sense. But this was an exception to the rule. As a general rule, I believe the Lord leads Christians to do that which is sensible by common sense standards.

F. CIRCUMSTANCES

Somewhat different is the problem of circumstances. Often, circumstances will suggest that a particular decision would be followed by unpleasant consequences, perhaps suffering. Yet the decision must be made and any unpleasant results must be endured, provided the decision is the Lord's will. Romans 12:2 tells us to stop being conformed to the pattern of this age. Yet the pressures of this age are great and tend to influence the Christian toward conformity to the world's standards instead of to God's standards. Circumstances may have the effect of putting pressure upon us to conform to the world, in which case they should be ignored. Yet at other times circumstances are meaningful and should be seriously considered in deciding about the Lord's will.

I think of a Christian accountant who was asked by his boss to be dishonest and juggle the accounts for the purpose of cheating on the income tax. He was told to do this or he would be fired. He refused to act dishonestly and was fired. Circumstances in this case—the threat of losing his job and being broke—were serious, yet had to be ignored in deciding that it was not the Lord's will to juggle the accounts. He made the right decision, although this resulted in some distressing circumstances. He lost his job.

On the other hand, I can recall a pastor who went to a church and faithfully preached the Word for many years and yet ended up by leaving that church. The circumstances here were the hostility and resistance of the people toward the Bible and toward the pastor for his insistence upon preaching the Word of God. Circumstances favored the decision to leave and work elsewhere. In such a case the Lord's will was for him to leave, for the Lord wanted to use him elsewhere. The circumstances were part of God's way of causing him to reach the right decision. Yet it might be that in a different church the same circumstances could be present but the Lord's will could be for the pastor to stay.

Whether circumstances are ignored or considered as crucial, the Christian is not to walk by sight but by faith (II Cor. 5:7). Circumstances should always be viewed as part of God's over-all plan. God is the ultimate primary cause behind the circumstances and He can either use them to a good purpose or He can overrule them, as He pleases.

Something should be said about the matter of "putting out the fleece." As used today, the term refers to the device whereby a Christian attempts to discern the Lord's will by the use of some visible, tangible sign or event. For example, the Christian who is struggling with the decision about whether to give a large amount of money to the church in a certain month may say to God: "Lord, if it is your will for me to give this large sum of money, indicate it by granting me huge success in my business for the next two days—success that is almost miraculous. If I don't have such success, I'll know it is not Your will." So, the Christian asks God to indicate a yes-or-no answer by performing some sort of semi-miraculous act. But this procedure is not exactly sound. What if God had already planned to grant huge success for the next two days for some other reason?

This device is supposedly based upon the experience of Gideon, who put out the fleece twice (Judges 6:36-40). Please notice what happened in this section of Scripture. God had previously told Gideon that he was going to liberate the Jews from domination by the Midianites, that God was with him and would grant him success. God had told him this several times and had told him to go ahead with his attack (Judges 6:12, 14, 16). Yet Gideon doubted the Lord. He doubted that God would do what He had promised. He was uncertain about whether he should go ahead and attack the Midianites or not. Doubting the truth of what God said, Gideon then asked for a sign from God. In Gideon's case the asking for a sign was something evil, for it stemmed from unbelief and it suggested that God might not be truth-

ful. Zacharias asked for a sign because of unbelief and was
stricken dumb because of so doing (Luke 1:18-20). Christ
said that it was an evil generation that sought for signs, indicating their unbelief (Matt. 12:39). Christ, when tempted
in the desert, indicated (Luke 4:12) that the Law of Moses
prohibited testing God (Deut. 6:16). To ask for a sign is to
test God to see if His word is true.

Gideon indicated in his request that he knew exactly what
the Lord's will was, although he lacked courage to carry it
out. (See Judges 6:36: "If thou wilt save Israel by mine
hand, *as thou hast said";* see also 6:37, 39.) So, putting out
the fleece had nothing to do with discerning the Lord's will.
God's will had already been revealed.

So today I cannot recommend the procedure of putting
out the fleece. It is entirely unnecessary, due to the omnipotent power of God the Holy Spirit. The Spirit is fully competent to communicate to us the will of God, without having
to resort to the use of signs, especially signs that are of a
semimiraculous or miraculous nature. Those who are led
by the Spirit (Rom. 8:14) and who utilize the information
and signposts available for guidance will find that there is no
need for special signs.

G. PEACE OF GOD

I have put this signpost near the end of the list because it
should have the final say-so. In Colossians 3:15 Paul commands us to "let the peace of God rule" in the heart. The
word for "rule" here literally means to "act as umpire." It
was the verb used for the calling of the decisions at an athletic
game. Today we have umpires who call the decisions at ball

games. Thus, we are to let the peace of God call the decisions in our life.

What is the peace of God referred to here? After one has tried diligently to fulfill as best he can the prerequisites and has considered all the signposts, he will find that he has a certain peace of mind about that particular decision which is the Lord's will. He will develop a conviction about a certain decision and this will be it. He will feel more strongly about that decision. He will have peace about it.

This feeling of peace may not be a reliable indicator if the prerequisites and other signposts have been badly neglected. The prerequisites and signposts act as a check on our tendency to have peace about that which we want in contrast to what God wants, which tendency might lead us astray in our judgment at times. This is one explanation for those mistakes in judgment made by Christians who claimed to have had peace when they made the decision. If we ignore the prerequisites and signposts, our mind may fool us into having a feeling of peace about something that represents our own way instead of God's way.

There are several verses in Romans that should be noted in connection with one's peace of mind regarding a decision about the Lord's will. In Romans 14:5 Paul talks about one man deciding that one day is more important (in a religious sense) than another, while a different man regards every day alike. He then says, "Let each be fully persuaded in his own mind." By this Paul urges that each man strive to think the problem through thoroughly, so that the conviction upon which he bases his behavior will be strong and sound. He does not want a man to be divided in his conviction, that is, to have doubt. Paul cautions against doubt in Romans 14: 23.

Now regarding the disagreement as to religious days in Romans 14:5, we must remember that both men cannot be right theologically. Both are right to obey their own consciences, but both are not right as to the decision made. One is right, having a strong, healthy (enlightened) conscience. The other is wrong, having a weak (ignorant, misguided) conscience. Everyone should obey his conscience, but he is also obligated to strive to see that the conviction is one of full persuasion and that all the facts are at hand. To be fully persuaded one has to investigate the facts, and this is exactly what the man with the weak conscience frequently fails to do. His conviction, not being based upon a thorough investigation of the facts and objective judgment, is not convincing. I believe it is hard for the man with the weak conscience to be fully persuaded. If he would be really honest with himself and with others, I believe he would have to admit that he actually isn't fully persuaded that he is right. Now, if one isn't sure, why not remain undecided until he can be sure? There is nothing wrong with saying, "I'm not yet certain," until one has more information and evidence.

Once a person has committed himself, it is hard to go back and admit that he made a wrong decision in the past. It is embarrassing. Nevertheless, as one grows in knowledge and maturity, it is inevitable that past errors of judgment will become obvious. These should be acknowledged and corrected.

I think I should say something about one Christian having peace of mind or doubt about the decision in another Christian's mind. I don't believe that one person can think for another. We all must do our own thinking. We can have an opinion about the decision that some other person makes and we can have doubt about it. But it is extremely difficult for one to be absolutely sure that it is wrong, unless the other's decision clearly violates some Biblical principle. You can't be sure what decision you would make unless you are in the shoes of the other person making that decision. If the shoe were on your foot, you might react quite differently than you think you would, as you think now about the problem only as an outsider. So we need to give other people the benefit of the doubt, unless the Scriptures have been violated.

To summarize, if the Christian has diligently tried to satisfy all the prerequisites and observed all the signposts, then that decision about which he has peace of mind will most likely be the Lord's will for his life.

H. RESULTS

I have mentioned results as a signpost because they give us some help in checking on our accuracy of discernment. They logically come last. Notice that circumstances sometimes are important in making a decision about the Lord's will before one acts. Results sometimes are important after one has acted, to check back on the decision.

Checking back on one's decision after action has been taken often becomes important, due to the necessity for a new decision as to whether to continue in the same course of action or to alter course. Sometimes, after starting in one direction, the Lord indicates that one is to change directions, and He may use results to help reveal this change of orders.

Results are hard to evaluate and one must be cautious.

Sometimes the final evaluation of results has to be delayed
for a long time, until finally the end results prove conclusive-
ly whether or not the decision was a correct one. An example
was Christ's earthly ministry. At first the results seemed very
poor, in that only a few responded positively, and they were
somewhat unreliable when danger came. But out of the limited ministry of these few disciples developed the Church,
which grew in numbers and power. So, the end results proved
that Christ was correct.

Moreover, if results seem good, this is not always proof
that the decision was correct. Likewise, bad results may or
may not be proof that the decision was wrong. Results by
themselves may not prove anything at all. For example, the
evangelist who uses various kinds of emotional gimmicks to
get a few more to come down to the front and make a profession of faith in Christ may get some results. Some people
may come down to the front. But why do they come
down? If the power of the Gospel of Christ does not
reach such people, and if it is necessary to manipulate them
psychologically in order to get them out of their seats, then
the religious profession that results is certainly doubtful as to
its authenticity. A crowd of people milling around in front
of a preacher, claiming they want to be Christians, looks
good. But unless their professions of faith are genuine, it
really means nothing except that they have had an emotional
experience.

One rule I will give: When results seem poor, one should
check back over the checklist of prerequisites to see if he
failed to qualify on one or more of them. If he ignored a
signpost or badly failed to satisfy a prerequisite, he can no
longer claim that his decision was sound.

If one has satisfied all prerequisites and followed all signposts and yet the results suggest he is on the wrong track, I suggest he go very slow in altering his decision. Poor results initially may be only a test from the Lord, and better results will eventually follow. If results get so bad that one is forced to alter his direction of action, he may consider that the Lord has used such circumstances to effect a change. God does have the right to change His orders whenever He pleases.

Take the case of a pastor who, after going to a church and trying as best he can to preach the Word and minister effectively among his flock, fails to make an impact upon the people. He finally gives up in despair and seeks another ministry. His results were obviously poor. But then God perhaps wanted him there in that place for a limited time, then wanted him to move somewhere else later.

Also, one must make a distinction between what results he wants and those results that God has planned. God has not planned that every pastor's ministry be wildly successful. The Apostle Paul preached in some villages where no one accepted the Gospel, yet it still was the Lord's will for him to preach there. Results that we consider poor may be viewed differently by God.

Now as to irrational doubts that come after or while a decision is being made, these doubts are usually related to a psychological problem, such as an overly strict conscience. (See previous discussion in section on emotional maturity.) The fear of criticism makes such a person reluctant to trust his decisions. Criticism to him is so painful emotionally that he must avoid it at all costs. So, he either can't decide and doesn't act at all, or after he has decided and acted he then becomes afraid he will be criticized and begins doubting his decision. He cannot logically and rationally evaluate his results, but only vacillates back and forth between different opinions, never being quite sure.

In spite of the difficulties involved, results must be inspected and evaluated, to keep checking on oneself. In this way one can stay in the center of God's will by taking corrective action when indicated.

Chapter 5

WHAT ABOUT DOUBTFUL THINGS?

HERE WE COME to the problem area of so-called doubtful things. This includes all things that are doubted as perhaps not acceptable to the Christian standard. The list of such things varies, depending upon what part of the country one lives in, upon what church one attends, upon how enlightened one is Biblically, and upon one's own unique emotional needs and prejudices. There is a frequent tendency for each Christian to think that his list is the only really accurate list and therefore should be authoritative for everyone else. This is unsound. It includes everything from chewing gum, alcohol, and cigarettes to football games, dancing, and television.

First, I want to caution Christians. I do not believe that a Christian should give up any and every activity that some other person casts doubt upon. It is not that simple. Just because some other Christian disapproves of that which you allow yourself to do does not necessarily mean that you are going to cause him to stumble. It is a mistake to try to apply such a principle to the areas of realistic disagreement that exist among Christians. Many Christians differ in their convictions as to what activities are permissible on Sunday. It is hard to be dogmatic about this particular issue. It is totally unrealistic for a Christian to aim at pleasing everyone so as not to displease anyone. There will always be some people who will criticize your actions.

The Bible does give us certain principles to help in making such decisions. Each person must evaluate his behavior in the light of these principles, and then make his own individual list of things that he believes are unacceptable before the Lord. He should then try to avoid those things. Furthermore, he should courageously stick to his own convictions and not let his conscience be bound by someone else's opinion.

Moreover, one should keep an open mind so that new wisdom may be acquired. As one grows in wisdom, it would be inevitable that the list should be revised from time to time to make it more accurate. In evaluating these things, one should have a good reason before he decides to partake or not to partake. We need a sound basis for the decision.

A doubtful thing is feared because it is thought that the Christian will be corrupted or defiled if he partakes of it. These doubtful things, being inanimate objects, usually are neither good nor evil. Generally, they have no power of evil in themselves (Rom. 14:14; Mark 7:15). Frequently, it is something about the person using it or the way he uses it that results in evil. Christ pointed out that evil proceeds from a man's heart (Matt. 15:18-19), not from the mere act of using something (Matt. 15:20). Whether or not something should be forbidden for the Christian depends upon the effect produced by its use. What response does it evoke from the heart? What effect does it have upon one's spiritual life? What effect does it have physically or psychologically? How does it affect others? These are the important issues.

So there are a number of questions by which one can test any doubtful thing. It is good to use this as a checklist in evaluating uncertain things. We are obligated to test these things and use only the good (I Thess. 5:21). God wants only the best for us and He allows us complete liberty to do that which is good. By good I refer to that which is honoring to God and edifying to us.

A. WHAT IS YOUR MOTIVE FOR DOING IT?

Sometimes one's motive for wanting to do something can be an important deciding factor. James condemned those who kept on asking (in prayer?) for something, yet did not receive it because they were asking for themselves evilly, so that they might spend it in their (lustful) pleasures (James 4:3, expanded translation). For instance, do you want to buy a Cadillac car because it really is an excellent car and you have the money and you need a car like that in your business? Or are you buying it out of pride, so everyone will look at you with admiration? Are you buying it for prestige? Are you trying to keep up with your neighbors? Pride is one thing we are warned against (Prov. 16:5; I John 2:16).

Is your motive appropriate for what you want to do? For instance, are you, a teen-age Christian, going to the high school dance because you have thought it over, concluded it not improper and simply enjoy dancing? Or is it that you really don't care to go, yet you resent your overly strict or overcontrolling mother and therefore want to go just to spite her? This is hardly a good reason to go. If you feel that your mother has done something improper for which you are justified in feeling resentful, the appropriate way to express this is to tell her about it.

My point here is that one should try to evaluate his own motives and become aware of the real reasons behind his actions. One has to do this to curb improper or inappropriate motivations.

B. IS IT GOOD FOR YOU?

In I Corinthians 6:12 Paul says that all things are lawful but not all things are profitable. We should try to anticipate what effects may result from our participation in the doubtful activity. Remember that we are to maintain our bodies and minds in the best condition possible so that we can be used by the Lord. In II Corinthians 4:7 Paul mentions that the treasure (of ministering the Gospel, in Paul's case) is in an earthen (clay) vessel. This means that God deliberately chose to use imperfect and vulnerable human beings for service, in spite of the fact that our weaknesses hinder us from more effective service. A physical disease or a mental disturbance makes us less efficient and effective in carrying out the Lord's will. So one should not do that which might make him less efficient and effective.

For example, we all need some recreation and pleasure in order to remain physically and emotionally healthy. For this reason, God has given us some things on earth to enjoy (I Tim. 6:17). If we fail to get enough of this, we become less efficient. If we get too much of it, we may become addicted to it and end up distracted from our work.

Thus, we must ask the question: Does it make the vessel more fit for service?

C. WILL IT ACT AS A THORN?

The scriptural basis for this test is the teaching by Christ in Mark 4:18-19 and Luke 8:14. Here Christ uses the common example of a good seed, the Word of God, which is planted in the ground, a man's heart. In this case He refers to the way in which the presence of thorns in the ground will hinder the growth of the seed and choke it off. The bad end result is that the Word of God does not produce the fruit in one's life that it could (Mark 4:19), and the Christian himself does not develop the spiritual maturity or produce the spiritual good works that he could otherwise.

These thorns are harmful. They must be avoided or one's spiritual life will be hindered. The Bible gives three general examples of thorns.

1. *Thorn of the "Anxious Cares of the Age"*
(Mark 4:19)

This thorn is called the "anxious cares [worries] of life" in Luke 8:14 . What does it refer to? In Luke the word for "life" is *bios* and refers to the necessities of everyday life. So, the reference here is to that worry that one may have about paying his monthly bills. It includes the house rent, food, utilities, and clothes. It also includes payments on the new car, new furniture, new refrigerator, television set, washing machine, insurance, toys, vacations, recreation, medical and dental expenses, and other items which are part of our everyday life.

It is easy to see how a man can become burdened with monthly payments that take every penny of his paycheck. If he has to struggle each month to make all his payments, perhaps worrying about bills that are overdue from last month, perhaps trying to figure out how he can still buy a new car, it is certain that this anxious concern over life's needs will act as a thorn. To have to think about such things very much uses up one's available mental energy. Instead of being occupied with the things of God, such a person tends to become preoccupied with the things of the world. God is gradually crowded out of his thoughts, and his spiritual condition gradually deteriorates.

So the Christian should ask himself a question whenever he is considering buying something. Is the purchase and use of this going to put me under such a financial strain that I might become anxious about my bills? If you can buy and use the item without developing an anxious preoccupation over it, you have passed the thorn test.

For instance, if your income fluctuates, dropping in the summer so that you couldn't make payments on a new car, perhaps it would be better to wait until you are more financially able. It is common to find people depressed and worried over bills they owe. Yet it is often their own fault because they try to buy too much too fast. The secret is to avoid getting into a situation that involves such financial pressure.

2. *Thorn of "Deceitfulness of Riches"* (Mark 4:19)

This thorn is called the "wealth of life" in Luke 8:14. It refers to the effect money can have upon a person. The Bible clearly says that covetousness (literally, love for money) is a root of all kinds of evil (I Tim. 6:10). This same verse describes the state of those who, moved by covetousness, go after money. Those who reach out for money are "led astray from the faith and pierce themselves through with many consuming griefs" (literal translation of I Tim. 6:10). Men are known to commit any kind of crime for the sake of money, such as robbery, assault and murder. Sometimes loss of money results in serious mental depression. One often wants more money than he has and is chronically frustrated and dissatisfied.

To set out to become rich just to have a lot of money is a poor goal in itself. To the person under pressure, worrying about the "anxious cares of the age," a lot of money may seem to be just what he needs. But this is very deceptive. Money doesn't usually bring happiness by itself. If one wishes to have a large sum of money in order to carry out a specific worthy goal, this may be acceptable. To provide one's family with a comfortable and happy life, is, of course, a reasonable goal. But just where does one draw the line as to what is necessary or unnecessary? useful or extravagant?

A person's heart can be drawn aside from spiritual things to a preoccupation with money. Paul pointed out two dangers always present after one has become wealthy: First, the rich person may become proud. He may erroneously think he is better than someone else because he has earned more money. He may become stuck-up. Second, there seems to be an inherent tendency in man to trust in riches. Although riches are clearly called uncertain (I Tim. 6:17) and perishable (I Peter 1:18), people still tend to fix their hope upon wealth. Money in such a case is very distracting. It becomes too important to a person. It has a way of requiring more and more of a person's time, energy and attention.

So one is obligated to consider the effect of money before making a decision about the Lord's will for his life. Perhaps an opportunity is available to make a million dollars. Would it always be the Lord's will? Not necessarily so. In fact, if one would be likely to become harmfully preoccupied with money as a result of success in the opportunity, it would not be the Lord's will. Many people are not able to have wealth without becoming preoccupied with it. Such people should leave it alone for the sake of their spiritual welfare. Other people can have wealth and yet remain unaffected. If you can handle a large amount of money without being adversely affected by it, then an opportunity to make a large amount may be acceptable within the Lord's will for your life.

3. *Thorn of "Pleasures"* (Luke 8:14)

In Mark 4:19 this thorn is listed as the "lusts for the remaining things," meaning those other than ordinary necessities of life. Things that are sources of pleasure for us can act as thorns if our enjoyment of them becomes too extensive and too important. If we become addicted to them, if we get to where we cannot be happy without them, then they are acting as thorns. Pleasures have a way of coming to seem like necessities to us.

I do not refer to the normal, average amount of recreation or pleasure which everyone should enjoy in order to live a balanced life. We should thank God for such recreation (I Tim. 6:17).

Rather, I refer to that tendency to become more and more preoccupied with the pursuit of pleasure. One can become dissatisfied with one or two vacations a year, then develop a need to take four or five vacations a year. One may become dissatisfied with only one or two recreation times a week and want one every day. Pleasures tend toward getting more of our interest and attention than is good for us, if we're not careful. As our interest shifts more in the direction of pleasures, we seem to need pleasures more and more and we gradually lose interest in the things of God.

The answer is to restrain oneself carefully and intelligently in the pursuit of recreation. Paul said not to use the things of this world in an unrestrained manner (I Cor. 7:31).

4. *Result of Cultivation of Thorns*

There is a progression in this process described in Mark 4:19. First, one worries about his daily needs, the necessities of life. Then he begins thinking that money is the answer to his needs. The more money he makes, however, the more he wants. As he is able to afford more things, he seems to develop a need for more things. Then he finds himself thinking of pleasures which money can afford.

The result is that the Christian's time, energy, and attention will be used up by preoccupation with worries, riches, and pleasures. A person involved in the pursuit of pleasure tends not to invest himself in the things of God. He tends to lose interest in the Word of God, with the inevitable lack of growth in maturity and deterioration in spirituality.

The principle holds true that one must invest himself before he can expect fruit in return. These thorns must be uprooted before the spiritual life can prosper, and before God's will can be accomplished to the fullest.

D. WILL IT ACT AS A WEIGHT?

I have made a distinction between thorns and weights. Thorns refer to those things which usually have the characteristic effect of choking out the Word of God and stifling our spiritual life. They always tend to do this and thus always have to be uprooted whenever they are discovered. In this sense they have a flavor of being bad. The Bible mentions three thorns: worries, deceitfulness of riches, and pleasures (Mark 4:19; Luke 8:14).

Things that become weights are neither good nor bad. They are activities that are perfectly all right in themselves, yet are not profitable for us spiritually because of the way they are used. The use of them may not lead us into sin, yet neither does it lead us into anything useful spiritually. They do hold us back by consuming our time and energy. They are like excess baggage; they hinder our progress. They are lawful but not profitable (I Cor. 6:12). So the question to be asked is not, What's wrong with it? but, Is it good for me?

The verse which commands us to lay aside every weight is Hebrews 12:1. Here we are told to lay aside the weights so that we can run with patient endurance the race, the race being our Christian career and life on earth. Certainly if we try to run while burdened down with useless weights, we will tire easily and quickly and will fall short of endurance.

A weight slows us down and tires us out. No one receives a prize for carrying around a weight, but for running a race swiftly and efficiently. A good example of this problem is the one mentioned in II Timothy 2:3-4, where it is said that a soldier who is going out to fight does not become entangled in civilian business affairs. Becoming preoccupied with business matters makes one less effective as a soldier. The lesson is that one shouldn't become too preoccupied with nonessential matters for fear of becoming less effective in his Christian walk.

In I Corinthians 9:26, Paul said he ran, but not uncertainly. By this he meant that he did not run in a direction that was not profitable, thus wasting his time and energy. Paul said he fought, but not as beating the air. He did not direct his blows at nothing. He used his energy in efforts that were goal-directed.

We discover what things in our lives are weights as we take stock of how we are running and try to run more effectively. Then we find ourselves being slowed down by something in our lives. As one casts aside something that is a weight, God is able to make him become aware of still another weight that may be present. As the weights drop off, it becomes easier to run the race.

Perhaps a specific example is in order: Perhaps you are considering joining a book-of-the-month club. Now, if you read these books as part of a normal amount of recreation, then this reading is a good means of relaxation and can be spiritually profitable for you. On the other hand, if you already have sufficient recreation, the addition of such reading may crowd out of your life some spiritually useful activity. In such a case, the reading could become a weight. If so, it would not be the Lord's will to join the book club.

E. IS IT AN ENSLAVING HABIT?

In I Corinthians 6:12 Paul states that he will not be brought under the power of anything, even though it may be lawful. If one is enslaved to something, he has suffered a loss of self-control. And self-control is absolutely necessary for one to know and do the will of God.

Peter warns us that the actions of a man's life prove who his master is (II Peter 2:18-19). If his life is characterized by sin and pleasure, then he is dominated by the same. Peter says that a man becomes enslaved to that by which he has been overcome. (See I Peter 2:19.) Thus, the glutton is enslaved to his appetite. When one repeatedly gives in to an

enslaving habit, he seems to end up dominated by that habit.
Paul says that one becomes a slave to that to which he yields
himself (Rom. 6:16). He then urges us to yield ourselves to
God (Rom. 6:13, 19). In order to direct one's life into
obedience to God one has to have self-control. This means
not being enslaved to things.

Paul says something useful in I Corinthians 9:27: "I treat
my body harshly and I make a slave of [my body], lest by any
means, although having preached to others, I myself should
become rejected [that is, disqualified for the prize]" (a literal, expanded translation). By harsh treatment he does not
refer to senseless physical mistreatment of one's body, such
as flagellation, as if to subdue it. Nor does he refer to in-
discriminate denial of one's wish or need to enjoy a pleasur-
able thing. He does not suggest that we live a life of poverty
and suffering, denying ourselves any pleasure. This would be
the extreme of asceticism, which is theologically unsound and
psychologically undesirable.

Rather, he means that whenever denial of a wish becomes
necessary in order to maintain good self-control or to avoid
spiritual harm, he denies himself gratification of that wish,
even though the denial might cause physical or emotional
discomfort. For example, one who, because of being over-
weight, goes on a reducing diet finds that while dieting the
body and emotions seem disturbed. He may feel weak and
irritable. Yet in order to maintain control and avoid en-
slavement to his appetite for food, the person perseveres in
his diet in spite of the discomfort.

A person can become addicted to anything. Thus, one
should avoid those things which would tend to enslave him,

so that he can remain free to do the will of God, unhindered by addictions.

F. WILL IT CAUSE A BROTHER TO STUMBLE?

This is the negative aspect of edification. "Edify" means to build up. The scriptural example given by Paul in I Corinthians 8:1-13; 10:6-7 refers to the practice of some Christians who continued to attend pagan banquets held in the idol temples. At these banquets the food was first offered in sacrifice to the idol, after which it was eaten. Although the Christian might go only for the good food and social life, yet by his presence he would also participate in the worship of a pagan god and thus give the false impression to others that such pagan worship was proper for Christians. By his action he might influence another Christian into mistakenly worshiping a pagan god.

An important principle in this test is whether or not a brother will see you or know about it. Indeed, God always sees us and knows what we are doing. But suppose one considers a certain activity not improper before God, yet a second Christian thinks it is wrong. Perhaps the second Christian is mistaken, having a conscience that is misinformed (weak). If one does that which seems wrong to the second Christian who is then persuaded to do it also, even though he still doubts it, then he has been caused to stumble in that he has been led to act against his conscience. So it is good not to do anything that causes a fellow Christian to stumble (Rom. 14:21). But it is also good to help the Christian with the weak conscience gain more knowledge so his conscience can become a more accurate guide.

One must avoid extremes in trying to apply this principle
of not offending one's brother. One must not let his life become enslaved to the unique convictions of other Christians.
Many Christians seem to disapprove of many things that
really are quite harmless. There are many, many things of
which some Christians disapprove. To avoid doing anything
which would "offend" any Christian would mean living a
severely restricted life. We are not obligated to so restrict
our lives according to the misconceptions of ignorant Christians. One should investigate to see if there really is danger
of a fellow Christian being stumbled before restricting his
life.

Furthermore, if you feel free to engage in the activity
which your Christian brother forbids for himself and if you
can indulge quietly, there is nothing wrong with your pri-
vate enjoyment of the activity. As long as you don't doubt it
yourself, you are free to enjoy it, giving thanks to the Lord
who provided it (I Tim. 4:4-5).

There also needs to be a response to the lack of knowledge
of the weak (misinformed) brother. He forbids something
that he would allow if his conscience were better educated.
You, his fellow Christian, also have an obligation to educate
him and help correct his distorted conception of Christian
morality.

It is important to be willing to let other Christians hold
to their own convictions without criticizing them. One can
discuss the problem in a friendly way without being critical.
This is especially true of doubtful things, about which it is
hard to be dogmatic. Paul commands us to stop such criticism
(Rom. 14:3-10).

G. WILL IT EDIFY YOUR BROTHER?

This is the positive aspect of edification. Will your action influence your brother in the right direction? Paul says we are to do that which is edifying to one another (Rom. 14: 19; I Cor. 10:23; I Thess. 5:11).

This principle is sometimes difficult to apply. Suppose, for instance, that the action which seems best for your brother is that of restoring a brother who has fallen into a trespass (Gal. 6:1). This is always an unpleasant task. Most people tend to get angry when someone points out a sin, an error, to them. Yet sometimes this correction is what they need most. So when one sees his brother sinning, he must consider whether it would be edifying to confront him with his sin. Sometimes it will do some good, and sometimes it will only make matters worse. It must be done in the right way and at the right time and by a person whose own spiritual ability and testimony are such that he is qualified to rebuke the sinning Christian (Gal. 6:1).

The principle seems easy to apply when it involves doing something pleasant for someone. However, even here one must stop and think the matter through. It is possible that doing something for someone might not be good for them. For instance, if that person is reluctant to be independent and self-responsible and has a tendency to get others to do his work for him, then doing something for him might result in further encouragement to him to continue being irresponsible. It might do him more good to insist that he do for himself. What the Christian brother wants is not the only thing to be considered. One must also consider what he needs. In Romans 14:19 Paul points out that both goals, peace and edification, are equally important. We should not overemphasize one at the expense of underemphasis of the other.

H. DOES IT COMPROMISE SEPARATION?

In II Corinthians 6:14-18 God commands us to be separate from unbelievers and from pagan worship. We are told to "stop becoming unequally yoked" with unbelievers (6:14), to "come out from the midst of them and be separate" and "stop touching the unclean thing" (6:17). Exactly what is forbidden here, and how should it influence our Christian life today?

The verb "to be unequally yoked" is *heterozugeō,* which means to be improperly yoked, or, more literally, "to be yoked with a different kind." The idea is illustrated in Deuteronomy 22:10 where the practice of plowing with an ox and ass together is forbidden. These two animals should not be yoked together and used for plowing as a team for several reasons. For one, the ass has a stride that is different from the ox, thus forcing the ox to walk in an unnatural way. The result is fatigue for the ox. Also, the ass frequently eats weeds along the way. The noxious odors stemming from this habit sicken the ox who, being so close to the ass, cannot avoid breathing in these irritating odors. The ox will become weak to the point where he is dragged along by the ass and may eventually die. The two animals are quite different in their natures and simply do not fit together.

In the Septuagint (Greek) version of the Old Testament, the noun form of this word (*heterozugos*) is found in Leviticus 19:19, where the Jews were commanded not to breed their cattle with a different kind (of animal). Thus, the idea was that an ox should not plow together with, or inter-

breed with any animal but his own kind. Christians then are
given a similar commandment. How does this prohibition
apply to our life today?

One certain application is that a Christian is not to marry
an unbeliever. This is emphasized in I Corinthians 7:39
where a widow is said to be free to marry again, but "only
in the Lord." In a marriage between a Christian and an unbeliever, the different sense of values (moral and otherwise)
existing in the two people creates a certain amount of incom-
patibility which results in marital discord. The unbelieving
partner is really not capable of advancing up to the higher
standard of the believer. He cannot change his nature (see
Jer. 13:23). Thus, unless the unbeliever should become a
Christian, the only resolution to the problem is for the believing partner to deteriorate down to the level of the unbelieving one. This is not a good solution, because it results in
a spiritual sickening and weakening of the Christian as he
labors under this improper yoke. He may be led into sin.
If instead the Christian remains steadfast and does not compromise his Christian principles and deteriorate, there is marital disagreement and dissatisfaction. Hence the unbelieving
partner feels somewhat uncomfortable and guilty living with
his Christian spouse. This situation can culminate in the unbelieving partner refusing to live up to his marriage vows,
resulting in separation and divorce. God recognizes this
problem in I Corinthians 7:15, where a divorce is permitted
if the unbelieving partner wishes it.

So, on the basis of this principle, one can say that it is never the Lord's will for a Christian to marry an unbeliever.
But this is not the only application for this principle.

What about working with an unbeliever on the job or in

some other type of endeavor? For instance, what if a Christian becomes a business partner with an unbeliever? Is this an unequal yoke? The answer lies in what type of business arrangement is made. If the partnership agreement is drawn up in such a way that the Christian is put in a position where he can be manipulated by his partner into doing something contrary to sound Christian principles, then it is an unequal yoke. The ox was subject to being helplessly dragged about by the ass. If the Christian in a partnership can be coerced or forced to do something improper, what are the possibilities for his response? He can remain steadfast and refuse to go along with it. But this causes conflict and discord with his partner. If he compromises and goes along with the improper actions of his partner, he is spiritually corrupted and weakened. He has been led astray into sin with its consequences (Gal. 6:7-8).

This problem of discord stemming from different moral convictions can exist in many situations where Christians participate with unbelievers in some activity. Now, in some situations the discord need not exist. It all depends upon whether the Christian is put under pressure to compromise his Christian principles.

What about having a time of social pleasure with unbelievers? If it doesn't result in pressure to compromise, then social contact in itself is harmless. In addition, such social contact is necessary to a certain extent if the Christian is to be a witness for Christ. It is necessary at this point to study some more principles of separation.

One important principle is given in Ephesians 5:11: "Stop having joint participation in the unfruitful works of the darkness, but rather even be rebuking [them] so as to bring conviction and confession" (literal, expanded translation). We are told here not to participate (along with unbelievers or anyone) in any activity that has the character of darkness. We must define what kind of works are unfruitful works of darkness. In the first place, the term "unfruitful" indicates that the work does not produce any good result; that is, good from the Christian standpoint. Not only is the effect of the work not good, but it may be spiritually harmful or dishonoring to God. Such unfruitful works are mentioned in the Bible in many places (see Gal. 5:19-21; Eph. 5:3-4; I Tim. 1:9-10).

These works have the character of darkness. Darkness is the opposite of light, and light is spoken of as that which is right according to the Word of God. The true and right stems from God. Moreover, anything untruthful or wrong does not come from God (I John 1:5, 6; 2:9, 11). To be in the darkness means to be ignorant of the truth. To walk in the darkness means to behave in a manner contrary to the truth. For instance, lying is contrary to the truth and thus of the darkness (Eph. 4:25).

Thus, a work of darkness is any activity which involves a violation of any truth or commandment of the Word of God. Notice in Ephesians 5:13 that these things (that is, the unfruitful works) are made manifest (that is, revealed as to their true character) by the light. The commandments to walk carefully as wise ones (Eph. 5:15) and to be understanding what is the Lord's will (Eph. 5:17) are logical at this point. It takes knowledge, wisdom, understanding and carefulness to avoid getting involved in a work of darkness.

We need to study the term "be separate" (II Cor. 6:17). It is *aphorizō*. It is related to the word *horizō,* to make a

boundary (*horos*) and to the word *apo,* from. The basic
meaning is to mark off from others by boundaries, to limit
off, to separate. Its meaning is clearly illustrated by its use
in Matthew 13:49 and 25:32. From this word we see
that there is to be a boundary line between Christians and
unbelievers that makes it possible to recognize that there
is a difference between the two. We are never to do anything
that results in a blurring of the line between Christians and
non-Christians. Peter says that after salvation we are not to
continue running together in a crowd (with unbelievers) in
the same excess of riot (literally, debauchery or abandoned
behavior) (I Peter 4:4). Paul tells us not to be participators
in the sins of others (I Tim. 5:22), and instead to depart
from iniquity (literally, to stand aloof from unrighteousness)
(II Tim. 2:19). Thus, there are many social activities (e.g.,
drinking parties, I Peter 4:3 and Rom. 13:13) which the
Christian has no business attending.

Furthermore, in regard to unbelievers, as a general rule we
are to turn away from (literally, shun) them (II Tim. 3:5)
in the sense of not having them as close, active friends. These
people, besides being ungodly in many ways (II Tim. 3:2-5),
also subtly wage an active campaign against Christianity
(II Tim. 3:6-8). Such people are our spiritual enemies.
This doesn't mean that we shouldn't be friendly and polite
to them, but it does mean we shouldn't have them for our
closest friends.

Especially are we not to participate in acts of worship
with unbelievers. Jude mentions how ungodly men tend
to creep in (literally, secretly slip in) to the church and
there spread corruption in the form of false doctrine (Jude

4). These people try to look like Christians but really are not (Jude 12, 19).

This large group of false Christians, organized into a false idolatrous religion, makes up part of what is called the great Babylon, the false religious system promoted by Satan on the earth (Rev. 18:2). This system is composed of all false religious groups. God has always wanted His people to separate themselves from this false group, and issues this command again for those of His people who are living on earth during the time of the great tribulation (Jer. 51:6; Rev. 18: 4).

As soon as the Church came into existence in the first century, certain problems arose. Some of the Christians continued to participate in feasts (banquets) where good food was served. They probably participated in order to enjoy the good food and to see some friends socially. Yet these feasts were held in honor of the false god (the idol), and the food was dedicated to the idol before being eaten. To a Christian it was just food and a social time, not religious worship. The idol or the food dedicated to the idol meant nothing to the Christian (I Cor. 8:4-8; 10:19). But the unbelievers did not have this knowledge (I Cor. 8:7; 10:20). To them it was real worship of what they thought was God and the feast was one of their forms of worship.

Thus, by participating in the feast the Christians were, in the eyes of the unbelievers, also participating in the religious worship. This wiped out the boundary line between Christian and non-Christian, and obviously was wrong. Paul condemns this practice strongly (I Cor. 10:20-22). James forbade it when he wrote to "abstain from pollutions of idols,"

meaning the articles of worship to idols, such as the food
served at the festival table in the idol temples (Acts 15:20,
29). The Lord Jesus Christ rebuked the church at Thyatira
because they tolerated the presence of a church member who
promoted the eating of things sacrificed to idols (meaning,
attending the pagan feasts held in the idol temple) (Rev. 2:
20).

Now, to buy the meat (previously sacrificed to idols) in a
public meat market, take it home and eat it was not improper
(Rom. 14:14; I Cor. 10:25). But it was wrong to eat it if
this meant participation in the idolatrous feast. The part of
false religion which involves such festivals is clearly called
idolatry (I Cor. 10:7).

To apply this to our present-day situation, one must realize that there are many churches today composed of people
who claim to be Christians yet deny the Bible both in doc-
rine and in practice. These people are not real Christians but
false brethren (II Cor. 11:26; Gal. 2:4). Their pastors are
not really ministers of God, but actually are activated by
Satan (II Cor. 11:13, 15). Their church services are dedicated, not to the true God, but to a false god conceived in
their own imagination, a god who doesn't really exist—an
idol. By this I refer to their concept of what God is like. The
Bible reveals what God is like. Yet these people reject the
Biblical concept of God and embrace instead a concept of
God which corresponds to what they want God to be like.
They conceptualize God as being what they wish Him to be
instead of as He is. Such a god as they conceptualize doesn't
exist, therefore their god is a false god or an idol. These
people resemble Christians outwardly but in reality deny God
(II Tim. 3:5). To participate with these people in their

worship is to participate in idolatry. Whenever a true Christian attends a worship service of these false Christians in a way that suggests that he shares the convictions of that group and is one of them, in their eyes he is participating.

Instead, the Christian is to maintain the boundary line between himself and unbelievers. This involves a separation from the religious activities of these false, idolatrous churches. To participate in them would make it appear that he and they were the same, as if both worshiped the same god, which is not true. In their eyes he becomes one of them when he participates with them. The fact that he, being a real Christian, knows better makes no difference. His obligation is not to participate with them but to rebuke them so as to bring conviction to them (Eph. 5:7, 11).

It is true that they will think you strange and uncooperative when you separate yourself, but this is unavoidable (I Peter 4:4). However, the act of separation does provide an opportunity for you to give a testimony for Christ (I Peter 3:15-16).

So before we participate in some activity, let us ask the question: Will this result in a blurring of the boundary line between Christian and unbeliever?

I. WILL IT LEAD YOU INTO TEMPTATION?

I must explain what I mean by temptation. A certain Christian may do well in the task of living a morally proper, spiritually sound life until he gets into a situation where he is enticed by bait. Bait may be anything he wants but shouldn't have (seductive women, illegal money). The presence of the bait arouses the latent desire, which desire then becomes transformed into a stronger one, lust (James 1:14). It was when Achan saw the bait, the garment and gold and silver which were forbidden but enticing, that he was stimulated to the point of coveting them, and then took them (Josh. 7:21). It is lust which, when the person gratifies it, gives birth to sin (James 1:15).

So bait has the effect of transforming a mild, harmless wish into lust. Now if one is not stimulated by the bait in the first place, he may avoid experiencing the lust and thus may avoid committing the sin. This is why it is perfectly legitimate for us to pray and ask God to help us avoid temptation (Matt. 6:13; Luke 11:4), meaning the avoidance of situations where bait is present that might stimulate us to lust.

For example, if you are a man prone to illicit sexual lust, you should avoid situations where a sexually seductive woman might tempt you. The bait (a seductive, flirtatious woman) will stimulate you sexually and you will experience lust. Such lust may result in your committing an illicit sexual act, a sin.

It is clear that God may help us avoid difficult situations where we may be tempted and provoked to sin. This is seen in Christ's command to Peter, James and John to be praying not to enter into temptation (Matt. 26:41; Luke 22:40, 46). In the garden of Gethsemane they were sleeping. Christ had warned them of the coming crisis when He would be seized by the Romans and crucified, and they, His disciples, might be threatened by the enemies of Christ (Matt. 26:31). Peter had claimed he would never deny Christ because of any such persecution (Matt. 26:33). But Peter was not as strong as he thought. He really was not ready for such a trial. So when the trial came He could not resist the temptation to deny Christ, which he did (Matt. 26:74-75). He could have avoided this failure by withdrawing from the scene of dispute, instead of following along to the place of Christ's trial. There was nothing that he could have done there anyway. He could do nothing to prevent the coming crucifixion. He would have done better if he had been home praying. Instead, sitting around in the midst of the enemies of Christ, he was pressured into acting in a way contrary to his beliefs.

It is true that any trial is an opportunity to remain faithful to Christ and be a testimony. But one must admit his own weaknesses. We all have weak spots (Matt. 26:41). Until one has made sufficient progress to where the specific vulnerability no longer exists, it is wise to avoid situations where one may be tempted in a weak area. In this way we can avoid some unnecessary failures.

J. DOES IT GIVE AN EXTERNAL APPEARANCE OF EVIL?

In I Thessalonians 5:22 Paul says to abstain from every form of evil. The word for form here is *eidos* and the usual meaning of this word is "outward appearance" (see Luke 9:29; II Cor. 5:7). It is also used in the sense of "kind" or "sort" (see Abbott-Smith's *Manual Greek Lexicon of the New Testament*). What does Paul mean here?

Perhaps the point he is making is to abstain from every kind of evil, such as sins of immorality, sins of greed, sins of dishonesty, sins of cruelty, and so forth. However, in the light of the numerous prohibitions against evil in the Bible, it seems somewhat superfluous to say every kind of evil. If we are to avoid evil, it goes without saying that this would include all kinds of evil. Furthermore, there are other Greek

words, such as *genos,* which are more commonly used to
mean "kind" or "sort" or "class" (see I Cor. 12:10, 28).
There must be a reason why Paul used this word, which emphasizes the external appearance.

It may be that Paul was putting an emphasis upon that
type of evil which does show on the outside. Not only are we
to avoid that evil which is inward, which others cannot see,
but we are to avoid anything which in its outward appearance
seems evil. The point may be that we are to notice what sort
of outward appearance results from our behavior.

For instance, if you believe that drinking alcoholic bever-
ages is wrong, then to be the operator of a liquor store or bar
would give a false impression. It would suggest to others
that you approved, rather than disapproved, of drinking.

Because we became holy (in a positional sense) when we
were saved (Heb. 10:10), we are now to aim at the goal of
holiness in our behavior (II Cor. 7:1; I Peter 1:15-16).
Thus, we are no longer to "fashion" ourselves according to
the pattern of our former lusts when we were ignorant of the
Gospel (I Peter 1:14). The word "fashion" here means to
assume an unnatural appearance, based on looks and behavior, according to a certain pattern. It is unnatural because it
doesn't fit the inner reality. The idea is close to our word
"masquerade." We are holy ones. We should not masquerade as unholy ones. The same word for "fashion" is used by
Paul in Romans 12:2 where we are told to stop being conformed to the pattern of this age.

The opposite problem exists in the case of false brethren
who "have a form of godliness" but prove their lack of real
Christianity by denying the power of godliness (II Tim. 3:
5). The word "form" here refers to a mere outward resem-

blance without the inner reality. These people may look like Christians but really are not.

On the other hand, real Christians sometimes look like they are not. They behave in a manner contrary to what would be expected of a Christian. So, we need to keep in mind how things will appear to others (Rom. 12:17).

K. DOES IT GLORIFY GOD?

In I Corinthians 10:31, Paul says that no matter what we permit ourselves to do, we should do all things for the glory of God. This means that everything we do should in some way result in glory to God (see also Col. 3:17, 23).

If we permit ourselves to enjoy a good musical program on television, can we do this in such a way that God will be glorified? Yes, we can. We can use this as a source of recreation, thank God for providing it, and thus keep our bodies and minds in good condition so that we can be used effectively by God. Thus, the activity enjoyed results in God being glorified by prayer, thanksgiving and service.

On the other hand, we can use such recreation in a manner unconnected with God. We can pursue such things too much, spending so much time seeking entertainment that we become addicted to it or perhaps distracted from our duties to God. One may find himself becoming overly concerned about self-gratification and less and less concerned about God. We need to have a proper balance.

We are told to be imitators of God (Eph. 5:1). The idea here is to demonstrate to others character traits that are like God's. The Christian who shows kindness to another is demonstrating the attribute of kindness. So, in contemplating our behavior, we should ask the question: Will this give others a false impression of what God is like? Will others become confused as to what a godly person is? When King David strayed and took Bathsheba as mistress and then wife, didn't this mar his image as a man of God?

So, by our behavior are we showing that we, as Christians, share in the holiness of God (Heb. 12:10; II Peter 1:4), or do we exhibit the imperfections of our own fallen human nature?

L. ARE YOU FULLY PERSUADED IN YOUR OWN MIND? (Rom. 14:5)

This is a final test. If you are persuaded that what you are doing is right and not wrong, don't doubt it when you do it. If you doubt it, and if your doubt doesn't stem from an abnormal and misinformed conscience, then you shouldn't do it (Rom. 14:23). What God wants is a heart that is obedient. The outward display of religious devotion is not nearly as important to God as the inner reality of devotion, manifested by obedience (I Sam. 15:22; Hos. 6:6; Matt. 12:7; Rom. 14:17).

The Bible indicates that it is a sign of blessedness (that is, spiritual prosperity) when a Christian does not doubt and criticize himself in regard to the things he permits himself to do and to enjoy (Rom. 14:22).

I would encourage each Christian to make final judgments only for himself, not for others. Paul points out that it is a mistake to decide a doubtful thing for someone else and criticize him if he doesn't agree with you (Rom. 14:10). However, one should be certain that the doubting is genuine doubting and not emotional quibbling. People who are emotionally unsure of themselves have a way of getting upset and becoming argumentative whenever someone else doesn't see things exactly as they see them. They want others to agree with them to relieve their own insecurity. We are not to be involved in such arguments (Rom. 14:1).

M. CONCLUSION

There are many things that different Christians consider doubtful, such as: movies, television, Sunday recreation, playing cards or dominoes, dancing, going to the opera or plays, swimming. The important point is that every Christian must evaluate these things for himself, using guidelines from the Bible. It is to God that we all must give an account (Rom. 14:10, 12). You can listen to the opinions of others, but you must make up your own mind from your own study of the Scriptures.

Chapter 6

SOME TYPICAL PROBLEMS IN DETERMINING GOD'S WILL

A. HOW FAR AHEAD (IN TIME) DOES GOD REVEAL HIS WILL?

LET US TAKE A SAMPLE PROBLEM: You are sure God has ordered you to be a missionary to Africa. You make all the necessary arrangements, except that you lack the money for transportation. You feel sure it is the Lord's will, and we shall assume that you are correct. The day before the boat leaves, you say to yourself, "Tomorrow I am going to leave on that boat, because I know God will send me the money somehow. It is His will that I go."

Now at this point you are on weak ground. You should have said to yourself, "Tomorrow I will leave on that boat, provided that tomorrow the Lord still wants me to go to Africa. Tomorrow, unless His will for my life has changed with new orders, God will somehow get the money to me so that I may buy my ticket. If I fail to receive the money and can't go, I will know that His will for me is something else." No doubt God would faithfully provide the money if it was His will for you to really go. But if the money didn't come in and you couldn't go, then had God let you down? Not at all. It would merely indicate a change of orders.

James makes it clear that one does not really know what will happen the next day (James 4:14). One should always say to himself, "I will do such and such tomorrow, provided the Lord is willing" (James 4:15; see Prov. 27:1).

So I don't believe that God does, in an absolute, irrevocable way, reveal His will for the next day or the next month or the next year. All that one can do is to act upon the conviction he has at that moment on that day. Since God is the Commander-in-chief, He has a right to issue new orders at any time.

This does not mean that one should not organize his efforts along some plan and try to prepare. To plan ahead is necessary in order to be effective and efficient. But keep in mind that one's plan should always be tentative, subject to change when so indicated. One shouldn't close his mind to any future change.

B. DOES GOD EVER CHANGE HIS MIND?

This question is closely related to the first one. God may seem to lead a person along one path, and then abruptly the door is closed and no further progress in that direction is possible. Has God changed His mind? Perhaps only His time schedule is different than you had anticipated it would be. However, what if it turns out that the door is truly closed permanently? Did God change His mind?

Hebrews 6:17 states clearly that God never changes His plan (*boulē*). The phrase "immutability of his counsel" literally means "the unchangeableness of His plan (*boulē*)." Romans 9:19 says that His will (*boulēma*, plan) is irresistible. However, God manifests different wishes (*thelēma*) at different times. One day, God may wish you to make plans

to go to Africa. The next day, He may wish you to go somewhere else. Although it seems that He is changing His mind,
actually He isn't. It is only that His plan includes different
goals.

In Acts 16:6-7 Paul, led by the Holy Spirit, was going
through Phrygia and Galatia, trying to go into Bithynia. But
orders changed and God did not permit him (to go into
Bithynia) (Acts 16:7). That night Paul received a vision
indicating a new direction in which to aim—Macedonia
(Acts 16:9-10). Seemingly God had changed His mind
about where He wanted Paul to go. Actually God had simply
unfolded a new chapter in His plan for Paul's life. From
the human point of view it did seem that God had changed
His mind. But doesn't the Commander-in-chief have the right
to issue changes in orders different from the preceding day?
The fact that Paul, before Macedonia, had been heading in a
different direction did not mean that Paul was out of the
Lord's will.

C. WHAT ABOUT AN APPARENT ACT OF
DISOBEDIENCE, YET SOME GOOD
RESULTS ARE SEEN?

Take the example of a Christian who wants to move to a
certain city, yet he knows that God has indicated that the
move is not His will. The man moves anyway—an act of
defiance. After he has lived in the city for awhile, even though
he has defied the will of God, yet one day he is instrumental
in leading another person to Christ.

Now, some people would say at this point that for God to
use this man in helping another to find salvation must mean
that the man really isn't out of the Lord's will. But this isn't

necessarily so. There are degrees of being in or out of the Lord's will. A Christian can still be used by God, even though he is defiant of God's will for part of his life.

How can God use such a Christian? God has chosen to work through vessels described as mud pots (II Cor. 4:7), which means that every Christian is going to be imperfect and disobedient to a certain extent. No one is perfect. If the Lord's work could be carried out only by perfect Christians, nothing would ever get done. There aren't any perfect Christians who are perfectly in the Lord's will for every part of their lives.

Now it is still true that the more completely one does obey God, the more God can use him. That man who defied the Lord and moved to a city of his own choosing would have found himself used by God much more if he had lived where God wanted him to live. He might have led hundreds to Christ instead of one. He might have won for himself many future rewards in Heaven if only he had obeyed. He might have delighted the Lord's heart much more by his obedience. God is especially delighted by those Christians who love Him enough to want to obey Him (I Sam. 15:22).

D. WHAT ABOUT AN APPARENT ACT OF OBEDIENCE, YET BAD RESULTS ARE SEEN?

Here, one must do several things. He must examine himself to see whether he was misled in his original conviction about the Lord's will. He may have been misled by some strong emotional feeling, by a lack of information about what the Bible teaches, or by something else. He must recheck the list of prerequisites and signposts.

Then, he must also realize that bad results may not really be bad. A lack of response to one's evangelistic preaching may be due to hardness of heart in the hearers, or to lack of preparation on the part of the preacher. Or it may be part of the plan of God, resulting ultimately in glory to God (II Cor. 2:15-16). God wants the Gospel to be preached. The sermon delivery of the preacher won't always be good. The response of the crowd listening won't always be good. But this doesn't mean that one was mistaken in thinking it was the Lord's will to preach that sermon.

E. WHAT ABOUT SOMEONE DECIDING THE LORD'S WILL FOR SOMEONE ELSE?

It just can't be done this way. Every man is responsible to the Lord and must decide for himself what is the Lord's will for his life (Rom. 14:3-5, 12; I Cor. 7:17-24). It is just as wrong for a Christian to announce that the Lord wants every Christian to be a foreign missionary as it is for one to say that no Christian should be a foreign missionary. Not all men have the same gifts (see I Cor. 12:4-11, 28-30).

At several different times in my life, friends of mine have received the call for me to become a medical missionary in a foreign land. But I've never received any such call. I've never felt convinced that God wanted me to do this. Instead, I have been called to do just what I am doing, practicing psychiatry here in the U.S.A.

Each person is to be fully persuaded in his own mind, not in someone else's mind (Rom. 14:5). Anyone who presumes to make an important life decision for some other Christian is encroaching upon the authority of God. God is the one who issues the orders. I am especially critical of those situations where bossy people are found trying to force their will on someone else. A common example is the parent who tries to make decisions for the grown son or daughter.

F. WHAT ABOUT WHEN CLEAR LEADING FROM GOD DOESN'T SEEM TO COME?

If this is a problem, the most likely answer is that you are negligent in the area of some prerequisite or guidepost. If possible, you should wait before making a decision until you can recheck the checklist and restudy the situation. Ask God to show you the area of difficulty. A frequent cause of uncertainty is an underlying wish to do something different from what God wants. But this is not the only cause.

If the time comes when a decision has to be made because of pressing circumstances, one has to make a decision, trusting that God will either guide into the right choice or will clearly show later on where one made the mistake. God does sometimes let us make mistakes so that a weak area of which we were previously unaware can be exposed. I suppose it is here that the idea of God's permissive will (a term not used as such in the Bible) fits in. God does sometimes permit us to make mistakes, but with the purpose of helping us become aware of weaknesses so that we can correct them. We all tend to make honest mistakes, but the mistake must be confessed to God, meaning that we must agree with Him that it was a mistake and we must profit from the experience.

Chapter 7

CONCLUSION

THE METHOD OF ASCERTAINING God's will which I have presented in this book is not perfect or infallible. This is because the writer, being an imperfect instrument, is not infallible. But by using this method the Christian can assume that he has correctly discerned God's will for his life with a fair degree of accuracy. When one makes a mistake, God is faithful to let him know about it (Phil. 3:15).

I believe that using an approach such as I have outlined should result not only in more accuracy but also in a greater feeling of assurance with less doubting. To the Christian who knows that he is in the Lord's will there is a feeling of contentment and security not possible otherwise. Indeed, in this world the safest place a Christian can be is where the Lord wants him to be.

By making a checklist I do not intend for the discernment of God's will to become a dry, boring, matter-of-fact procedure that one performs without any feeling. It is certainly a deeply spiritual performance, requiring all the love, devotion and wisdom that the Christian has available. My goal is rather to help my fellow Christians to be more accurate in their discernment of what God wishes of them.

We all wish to obey Him and to glorify Him. So let us use anything that will help us to be more efficient and effective vessels of the Lord.

Appendix

CHECKLIST FOR DETERMINING GOD'S WILL

I THOUGHT it might be useful to make a checklist which summarizes the main points in the book. One could quickly go over this list while considering a decision about the Lord's will.

1. Are you seeking to know about God's plan, which is secret and unchangeable? Or do you seek to determine what God wants for your life, which can be determined?

2. Is your physical condition good enough that you are not likely to make a mistake of judgment due to poor functioning of the brain?

3. Have you considered the possibility that your tentative decision may be influenced by a prejudice stemming from an area of emotional immaturity? Is the reasoning behind your decision really logical and appropriate?

4. In making your decision, are you using that wisdom which comes from God, which wisdom is used by the spiritually mature Christian?

5. Does your wish to know God's will stem from the desire to obey Him, which desire is characteristic of one who has once for all presented himself to God for service? Have you put God's way first before your own way?

6. Is there in your heart a sincere desire to know God's will? Do you really want to know?

7. On this particular day, when you are trying to make a decision about God's will, is your day-by-day willingness to obey at a sufficiently high level? Today, are you willing to take up your cross?

8. Are you willing to accept the authority of God's Word about this matter? Are you willing for this area of your life to be subject to the authority and control of God?

9. Are you trusting, by faith, that God will indicate to you the correct decision through the ministry of God the Holy Spirit?

10. Are you willing to pray about the decision and wait until the answer becomes clear?

11. If you are a new Christian and therefore relatively inexperienced, are you humble enough to realize that you must be all the more careful because of your inexperience?

12. Having studied a good translation and made an effort to determine the proper interpretation, have you diligently tried to utilize appropriate verses from the Bible in making your decision?

13. Have you noticed what you really want to do in your own heart?

14. Have you noticed what your conscience says about the issue? If you have doubt, is the doubt based upon an appropriate Biblical principle?

15. Have you considered the advice, if available, of your pastor or Christian friends?

16. Have you utilized all available knowledge that is pertinent to the matter and tried to incorporate this into your

process of reasoning about the decision? What would common sense say?

17. What do circumstances suggest? Are the circumstances such that they cannot be ignored?

18. Which decision do you have peace about?

19. Are there results which strongly suggest you ought to consider a new course of action?

20. What is your real motive for wanting to take this action?

21. Will the action taken result in something to your benefit?

22. Will it act as a thorn?

23. Will it act as a weight?

24. Will it result in your becoming enslaved to some undesirable habit?

25. Will it cause a brother to stumble?

26. Will it edify your brother?

27. Will it compromise separation?

28. Will it lead you into temptation?

29. Will it give an external appearance of evil?

30. Will it glorify God?

SCRIPTURE INDEX

SUBJECT INDEX